westermann

Stories of the Colonial and Postcolonial Experience

annotated
by Rudolph F. Rau

tasks
by Ilka Kratz

Materialien zum Download

Materialien für Lehrkräfte mit didaktisch-methodischen Hinweisen, Hintergrundinformationen und Lösungen zu den Aufgaben der Textausgabe finden Sie online auf www.westermann.de. Geben Sie dafür in das Suchfeld auf der Startseite die Nummer 73651 ein. In der Rubrik „Ergänzende Materialien" können Sie das Material abrufen.

Bildquellen

|Alamy Stock Photo (RMB), Abingdon/Oxfordshire: Cheese Scientist 37.2; Doak, Gary 38.1; Pictorial Press Ltd 37.1. |Getty Images (RF), München: Yeowell, Gary Titel.

Textquellen

5-10   "Shooting an Elephant" by George Orwell, in *The Collected Essays, Journalism and Letters of George Orwell*, Volume 1, Martin Secker & Warburg 1968.

11-27   "The Embassy of Cambodia" by Zadie Smith. Published by *The New Yorker*, 2013. Copyright © Zadie Smith. Reproduced by permission of the author c/o Rogers, Coleridge & White Ltd., 20 Powis Mews, London W11 1JN.

28-35   "My Son, the Fanatic" by Hanif Kureishi. Copyright © 1997 by Hanif Kureishi, used by permission of The Wylie Agency (UK) Limited.

40   *Burmese Days* by George Orwell, Harper & Brothers 1934.

48   "Modern slavery and public health" by Elizabeth Such, Claire Laurent and Sarah Salway, Government Digital Services, UK Government, https://www.gov.uk/government/publications/modern-slavery-and-public-health/modern-slavery-and-public-health#definition-of-modern-slavery, accessed 23 September 2020.

50   "Second Generasians" by Sarfraz Manzoor, in *Spotlight* 2/04, pp. 11-12.

westermann GRUPPE

© 2021 Bildungshaus Schulbuchverlage Westermann Schroedel Diesterweg Schöningh Winklers GmbH, Georg-Westermann-Allee 66, 38104 Braunschweig
www.westermann.de

Druck A⁵ / Jahr 2022
Alle Drucke der Serie A sind im Unterricht parallel verwendbar.

Redaktion: Thorsten Schimming, Angela Wesser, Emily Wilson
Layout: Harald Thumser, Frankfurt am Main
Druck und Bindung: Westermann Druck Zwickau GmbH, Crimmitschauer Straße 43, 08058 Zwickau

ISBN 978-3-425-**73651**-8

Contents

Introduction

This booklet contains the three short stories *Shooting an Elephant* by George Orwell, *The Embassy of Cambodia* by Zadie Smith and *My Son the Fanatic* by Hanif Kureishi.

After the short stories, you will find short biographies of the three authors (pages 37-38) and a lot of tasks to help you analyse the three short stories. There are pre-reading, while reading and post-reading sections for all three stories.

In addition, you will find general pre-reading tasks on pages 39-42 and general post-reading tasks on page 54.

The text of the three short stories is complimented by a wealth of useful annotations to help you understand both the language used and the deeper meaning of the text.

A list of literary terms and stylistic devices is provided on pages 55-56, which will help you in analysing the stories.

Biographies, tasks and literary terms can be easily separated from the rest of the booklet so that it can be used in exams.

Shooting an Elephant

by George Orwell (1936)

In Moulmein, in Lower Burma, I was hated by large numbers of people – the only time in my life that I have been important enough for this to happen to me. I was sub-divisional police officer of the town, and in an aimless, petty kind of way anti-European feeling was very
5 bitter. No one had the guts to raise a riot, but if a European woman went through the bazaars alone somebody would probably spit betel juice over her dress. As a police officer I was an obvious target and was baited whenever it seemed safe to do so. When a nimble Burman tripped me up on the football field and the referee (another Bur-
10 man) looked the other way, the crowd yelled with hideous laughter. This happened more than once. In the end the sneering yellow faces of young men that met me everywhere, the insults hooted after me when I was at a safe distance, got badly on my nerves. The young Buddhist priests were the worst of all. There were several thousands
15 of them in the town and none of them seemed to have anything to do except stand on street corners and jeer at Europeans.

All this was perplexing and upsetting. For at that time I had already made up my mind that imperialism was an evil thing and the sooner I chucked up my job and got out of it the better. Theoretically –
20 and secretly, of course – I was all for the Burmese and all against their oppressors, the British. As for the job I was doing, I hated it more bitterly than I can perhaps make clear. In a job like that you see the dirty work of Empire at close quarters. The wretched prisoners huddling in the stinking cages of the lock-ups, the grey, cowed faces of the long-
25 term convicts, the scarred buttocks of the men who had been flogged with bamboos – all these oppressed me with an intolerable sense of guilt. But I could get nothing into perspective. I was young and ill-educated and I had had to think out my problems in the utter silence that is imposed on every Englishman in the East. I did not even know
30 that the British Empire is dying, still less did I know that it is a great deal better than the younger empires that are going to supplant it. All I knew was that I was stuck between my hatred of the empire I served and my rage against the evil-spirited little beasts who tried to make my job impossible. With one part of my mind I thought of the Brit-
35 ish Raj as an unbreakable tyranny, as something clamped down, *in saecula saeculorum*, upon the will of prostrate peoples; with another part I thought that the greatest joy in the world would be to drive a bayonet into a Buddhist priest's guts. Feelings like these are the normal by-products of imperialism; ask any Anglo-Indian official, if you
40 can catch him off duty.

One day something happened which in a roundabout way was enlightening. It was a tiny incident in itself, but it gave me a better glimpse than I had had before of the real nature of imperialism – the real motives for which despotic governments act.

Moulmein [maʊlˈmaɪn] important port city
Burma part of British India since 1886, made a separate colony in 1937, independent since 1948, now called Myanmar
police officer Orwell himself was a police officer in Burma from 1922 to 1927.
petty [ˈpeti] small-minded
bitter *here:* strong
guts (informal) courage
betel [ˈbiːtl] Asian plant the leaves and nuts of which are chewed
to **bait** [beɪt] *here:* to deliberately try to make sb angry by making insulting remarks
nimble [ˈnɪmb(ə)l] able to move easily
to **trip** sb **up** *jdm ein Bein stellen*
to **look the other way** *wegschauen*
hideous [ˈhɪdiəs] very ugly or frightening
to **sneer** *höhnisch grinsen*
to **hoot** [huːt] to yell disrespectfully

to **jeer at** sb *jdn verhöhnen*

to **chuck up** (informal) to give up

oppressor *Unterdrücker*
at close quarters quite closely
wretched [ˈretʃɪd] miserable
to **huddle** to crowd together
lock-up jail • **cowed** made to feel afraid
convict prisoner
scarred *vernarbt* • **buttock** *Hinterteil*
to **flog** to beat, to whip

utter complete
to **impose** to force

a great deal a lot
to **supplant** to replace

British Raj [rɑːdʒ] British rule of India before 1947
to **clamp down** to hold down tightly
in saecula saeculorum (Latin) for ever and ever (often used at the end of a prayer)
prostate lying face down • **guts** *Eingeweide*
by-product *Nebenprodukt*
Anglo-Indian English person who has lived in India for a long time
off duty *dienstfrei*
enlightening *aufschlussreich*
glimpse *here:* insight

subinspector policeman of lower middle
rank

to **ravage** [ˈrævɪdʒ] to damage badly

elephant escaped (handwritten)

rifle [ˈraɪf(ə)l] *Gewehr*
in terrorem (Latin) as a means to frighten

tame *zahm*
must (Hindi) mad; quite normal behaviour
for tame male elephants, especially when
they are sexually excited
due expected
mahout [məˈhaʊt] (Hindi) keeper and driver
of an elephant
to **set out in pursuit** to try to find and catch

to **raid** *überfallen* • **stall** stand
to **devour** [dɪˈvaʊə] to eat quickly
stock the food the stall sold
municipal of the town
to **take to** one's **heels** to flee
constable [kʌnstəb(ə)l] policeman
quarter district
squalid [ˈskwɒlɪd] dirty and shabby
thatched covered • **stuffy** *stickig, schwül*
the rains monsoon, period of heavy rain
during the summer in South Asia
invariably always

thought that story wasn't true anymore (handwritten)

to **profess** (formal) to claim

scandalized cry cry expressing shock

switch thin, short stick

to **shoo away** *wegscheuchen*
to **click** one's **tongue** mit der Zunge
schnalzen
sprawling spread out • **mud** *Schlamm*
Dravidian [drəˈvɪdiən] member of a people
mainly native to southern India
coolie unskilled labourer working for low
wages, especially in the East
trunk *Rüssel*
to **grind, ground, ground** to press
to **score** to cut • **trench** *Furche*
foot 1 foot = 30.48 cm
yard 1 yard = 0.91 cm • **belly** stomach
crucified *gekreuzigt* • to **coat** to cover

unendurable *unerträglich*

Early one morning the subinspector at a police station the other end of the town rang me up on the phone and said that an elephant was ravaging the bazaar. Would I please come and do something about it? I did not know what I could do, but I wanted to see what was happening and I got on to a pony and started out. I took my rifle, an old 44 Winchester and much too small to kill an elephant, but I thought the noise might be useful *in terrorem*. Various Burmans stopped me on the way and told me about the elephant's doings. It was not, of course, a wild elephant, but a tame one which had gone "must". It had been chained up, as tame elephants always are when their attack of "must" is due, but on the previous night it had broken its chain and escaped. Its mahout, the only person who could manage it when it was in that state, had set out in pursuit, but had taken the wrong direction and was now twelve hours' journey away, and in the morning the elephant had suddenly reappeared in the town. The Burmese population had no weapons and were quite helpless against it. It had already destroyed somebody's bamboo hut, killed a cow and raided some fruit-stalls and devoured the stock; also it had met the municipal rubbish van and, when the driver jumped out and took to his heels, had turned the van over and inflicted violences upon it.

The Burmese subinspector and some Indian constables were waiting for me in the quarter where the elephant had been seen. It was a very poor quarter, a labyrinth of squalid bamboo huts, thatched with palm leaf, winding all over a steep hillside. I remember that it was a cloudy, stuffy morning at the beginning of the rains. We began questioning the people as to where the elephant had gone and, as usual, failed to get any definite information. That is invariably the case in the East; a story always sounds clear enough at a distance, but the nearer you get to the scene of events the vaguer it becomes. Some of the people said that the elephant had gone in one direction, some said that he had gone in another, some professed not even to have heard of any elephant. I had almost made up my mind that the whole story was a pack of lies, when we heard yells a little distance away. There was a loud, scandalized cry of "Go away, child! Go away this instant!" and an old woman with a switch in her hand came round the corner of a hut, violently shooing away a crowd of naked children. Some more women followed, clicking their tongues and exclaiming; evidently there was something that the children ought not to have seen. I rounded the hut and saw a man's dead body sprawling in the mud. He was an Indian, a black Dravidian coolie, almost naked, and he could not have been dead many minutes. The people said that the elephant had come suddenly upon him round the corner of the hut, caught him with its trunk, put its foot on his back and ground him into the earth. This was the rainy season and the ground was soft, and his face had scored a trench a foot deep and a couple of yards long. He was lying on his belly with arms crucified and head sharply twisted to one side. His face was coated with mud, the eyes wide open, the teeth bared and grinning with an expression of unendurable

dead body found ↓ supposed to be killed by elephant (handwritten)

agony. (Never tell me, by the way, that the dead look peaceful. Most of the corpses I have seen looked devilish.) The friction of the great beast's foot had stripped the skin from his back as neatly as one skins a rabbit. As soon as I saw the dead man I sent an orderly to a friend's
5 house nearby to borrow an elephant rifle. I had already sent back the pony, not wanting it to go mad with fright and throw me if it smelt the elephant.

The orderly came back in a few minutes with a rifle and five cartridges, and meanwhile some Burmans had arrived and told us
10 that the elephant was in the paddy fields below, only a few hundred yards away. As I started forward practically the whole population of the quarter flocked out of the houses and followed me. They had seen the rifle and were all shouting excitedly that I was going to shoot the elephant. They had not shown much interest in the elephant when
15 he was merely ravaging their homes, but it was different now that he was going to be shot. It was a bit of fun to them, as it would be to an English crowd; besides they wanted the meat. It made me vaguely uneasy. I had no intention of shooting the elephant – I had merely sent for the rifle to defend myself if necessary – and it is always
20 unnerving to have a crowd following you. I marched down the hill, looking and feeling a fool, with the rifle over my shoulder and an ever-growing army of people jostling at my heels. At the bottom, when you got away from the huts, there was a metalled road and beyond that a miry waste of paddy fields a thousand yards across, not
25 yet ploughed but soggy from the first rains and dotted with coarse grass. The elephant was standing eight yards from the road, his left side towards us. He took not the slightest notice of the crowd's approach. He was tearing up bunches of grass, beating them against his knees to clean them and stuffing them into his mouth.
30 I had halted on the road. As soon as I saw the elephant I knew with perfect certainty that I ought not to shoot him. It is a serious matter to shoot a working elephant – it is comparable to destroying a huge and costly piece of machinery – and obviously one ought not to do it if it can possibly be avoided. And at that distance, peacefully eating,
35 the elephant looked no more dangerous than a cow. I thought then and I think now that his attack of "must" was already passing off; in which case he would merely wander harmlessly about until the mahout came back and caught him. Moreover, I did not in the least want to shoot him. I decided that I would watch him for a little while
40 to make sure that he did not turn savage again, and then go home.

But at that moment I glanced round at the crowd that had followed me. It was an immense crowd, two thousand at the least and growing every minute. It blocked the road for a long distance on either side. I looked at the sea of yellow faces above the garish clothes – faces all
45 happy and excited over this bit of fun, all certain that the elephant was going to be shot. They were watching me as they would watch a conjurer about to perform a trick. They did not like me, but with the magical rifle in my hands I was momentarily worth watching. And

---

agony terrible pain
corpse dead body • **friction** Reibung
to **strip** to remove the outer layer of
orderly simple soldier without any special skills
elephant rifle large-calibre rifle whose bullets can pass through the thick skin of an elephant

cartridge Patrone

paddy field field planted with rice

to **flock out** to leave in great numbers

crowd was excited

merely only, just

uneasy anxious • **intention** Absicht
did not want to kill the animal
unnerving making you feel nervous
fool idiot • to **jostle** to push forward
at sb's heels close behind sb
metalled covered with small stones
miry ['maɪri] muddy
waste area that is boring to look at
to **plough** [plaʊ] pflügen
soggy soft and wet
dotted with übersät mit • **coarse** thick
slight small
approach coming closer • to **tear** reißen
bunch number of things held closely together

elephant was very calm and didn't do anything
to **pass off** here: to slowly decrease

savage ['sævɪdʒ] aggressive, violent
to **glance at** to look quickly at

immense very large

garish brightly, but unpleasantly coloured

conjurer person who performs magic tricks

crowd didn't like him because he was european but they were dependent on him high expectations

irresistibly *here:* with little possibility of resisting

to **grasp** to understand
hollowness ['hɒləʊnəs] lacking in real value, meaninglessness
futility [fjuːˈtɪləti] pointlessness
dominion control, rule • **piece** theatre play
puppet *Marionette*
to and fro back and forth
to **turn tyrant** to become a despot
hollow empty
to **pose** to play a part to impress others
dummy *Mannequin*
conventionalized stereotypical

sahib ['saːɪb] a form of address used by Indians for a European with some official or social status
resolute decisive, determined
to **trail away** to walk slowly away
feebly showing weakness

preoccupied very concentrated on sth
air *here:* manner of behaviour
squeamish ['skwiːmɪʃ] easily upset by sth unpleasant

a hundred pounds presumably British Pounds; would be worth several thousand Pounds today
tusk *Stoßzahn*

to **charge** to suddenly attack

a poor shot a person not able to aim well

toad *Kröte* • **steamroller** *Dampfwalze*

ordinary normal, usual

sole only   *important?*

suddenly I realized that I should have to shoot the elephant after all. The people expected it of me and I had got to do it; I could feel their two thousand wills pressing me forward, irresistibly. And it was at this moment, as I stood there with the rifle in my hands, that I first grasped the hollowness, the futility of the white man's dominion in 5 the East. Here was I, the white man with his gun, standing in front of the unarmed native crowd – seemingly the leading actor of the piece; but in reality I was only an absurd puppet pushed to and fro by the will of those yellow faces behind. I perceived in this moment that when the white man turns tyrant it is his own freedom that he 10 destroys. He becomes a sort of hollow, posing dummy, the conventionalized figure of a *sahib*. For it is the condition of his rule that he shall spend his life in trying to impress the "natives," and so in every crisis he has got to do what the "natives" expect of him. He wears a mask, and his face grows to fit it. I had got to shoot the elephant. I 15 had committed myself to doing it when I sent for the rifle. A *sahib* has got to act like a *sahib*; he has got to appear resolute, to know his own mind and do definite things. To come all that way, rifle in hand, with two thousand people marching at my heels, and then to trail feebly away, having done nothing – no, that was impossible. The crowd 20 would laugh at me. And my whole life, every white man's life in the East, was one long struggle not to be laughed at.

But I did not want to shoot the elephant. I watched him beating his bunch of grass against his knees, with that preoccupied grandmotherly air that elephants have. It seemed to me that it would be murder 25 to shoot him. At that age I was not squeamish about killing animals, but I had never shot an elephant and never wanted to. (Somehow it always seems worse to kill a large animal.) Besides, there was the beast's owner to be considered. Alive, the elephant was worth at least a hundred pounds; dead, he would only be worth the value of his 30 tusks, five pounds, possibly. But I had got to act quickly. I turned to some experienced-looking Burmans who had been there when we arrived, and asked them how the elephant had been behaving. They all said the same thing: he took no notice of you if you left him alone, but he might charge if you went too close to him. 35

It was perfectly clear to me what I ought to do. I ought to walk up to within, say, twenty-five yards of the elephant and test his behaviour. If he charged, I could shoot; if he took no notice of me, it would be safe to leave him until the mahout came back. But also I knew that I was going to do no such thing. I was a poor shot with a rifle and 40 the ground was soft mud into which one would sink at every step. If the elephant charged and I missed him, I should have about as much chance as a toad under a steamroller. But even then I was not thinking particularly of my own skin, only of the watchful yellow faces behind. For at that moment, with the crowd watching me, I was not 45 afraid in the ordinary sense, as I would have been if I had been alone. A white man mustn't be frightened in front of "natives"; and so, in general, he isn't frightened. The sole thought in my mind was that if anything went wrong those two thousand Burmans would see me pursued, caught, trampled on and reduced to a grinning corpse like that Indian up the hill. And if that happened it was quite probable that some of them would laugh. That would never do. There was only 5 one alternative. I shoved the cartridges into the magazine and lay down on the road to get a better aim.

The crowd grew very still, and a deep, low, happy sigh, as of people who see the theatre curtain go up at last, breathed from innumerable throats. They were going to have their bit of fun after all. The 10 rifle was a beautiful German thing with cross-hair sights. I did not then know that in shooting an elephant one would shoot to cut an imaginary bar running from earhole to earhole. I ought, therefore, as the elephant was sideways on, to have aimed straight at his earhole, actually I aimed several inches in front of this, thinking the brain 15 would be further forward.

When I pulled the trigger I did not hear the bang or feel the kick – one never does when a shot goes home – but I heard the devilish roar of glee that went up from the crowd. In that instant, in too short a time, one would have thought, even for the bullet to get there, a 20 mysterious, terrible change had come over the elephant. He neither stirred nor fell, but every line of his body had altered. He looked suddenly stricken, shrunken, immensely old, as though the frightful impact of the bullet had paralysed him without knocking him down. At last, after what seemed a long time – it might have been five seconds, 25 I dare say – he sagged flabbily to his knees. His mouth slobbered. An enormous senility seemed to have settled upon him. One could have imagined him thousands of years old. I fired again into the same spot. At the second shot he did not collapse but climbed with desperate slowness to his feet and stood weakly upright, with legs sagging and 30 head drooping. I fired a third time. That was the shot that did for him. You could see the agony of it jolt his whole body and knock the last remnant of strength from his legs. But in falling he seemed for a moment to rise, for as his hind legs collapsed beneath him he seemed to tower upward like a huge rock toppling, his trunk reaching skyward 35 like a tree. He trumpeted, for the first and only time. And then down he came, his belly towards me, with a crash that seemed to shake the ground even where I lay.

I got up. The Burmans were already racing past me across the mud. It was obvious that the elephant would never rise again, but 40 he was not dead. He was breathing very rhythmically with long rattling gasps, his great mound of a side painfully rising and falling. His mouth was wide open – I could see far down into caverns of pale pink throat. I waited a long time for him to die, but his breathing did not weaken. Finally I fired my two remaining shots into the spot where I 45 thought his heart must be. The thick blood welled out of him like red velvet, but still he did not die. His body did not even jerk when the shots hit him, the tortured breathing continued without a pause. He was dying, very slowly and in great agony, but in some world remote

to **pursue** to chase after

That would never do. That would not be acceptable.
to **shove** to push with force

sigh [saɪ] *Seufzer*
curtain *Vorhang* • **innumerable** very many

German thing a Mauser hunting rifle, widely used in Asia and Africa at the time
cross-hair sights *Zielfernrohr mit Fadenkreuz*
bar line
sideways on with the side towards me
inch 1 inch = 2.54 cm • **brain** *Gehirn*
to **pull the trigger** *abdrücken*
kick *Rückstoß*
to **go home** here: to hit the target
roar loud, deep cry • **glee** *Schadenfreude*
bullet ['bʊlɪt] piece of metal shot from a gun
to **stir** to move slightly
stricken deeply affected by pain
shrunken seemingly smaller
to **paralyse** sb: to make sb unable to move
to **knock** sb **down** to make sb fall
I dare say I think
to **sag** to sink because of weight
to **slobber** *sabbern*
settled upon him come over him

to **droop** to hang down
did for him finished him off
to **jolt** to give a sudden shock
remnant what still remained
hind [haɪnd] back
to **tower** to rise up high
to **topple** to become unsteady and fall over
to **trumpet** to make a loud sound through the trunk

to **rattle** *rasseln*
gasp short intake of breath
mound small hill • **cavern** *Höhle*

to **well out** to flow out
velvet *Samt* • to **jerk** to move suddenly
tortured with great suffering
remote far away

dreadful terrible

to **pour** here: to do sth continuously

dah long knife with a curved blade common in South Asia
basket Korb
to **strip** here: to remove the flesh
bone Knochen

powerless because he's an indian ⟶

it was a damn shame es war sehr bedauerlich

Coringhee from the seaport of Coringa in Madras, now Chennai

sufficient adequate · **pretext** excuse

1) George has more power than him because he's white

from me where not even a bullet could damage him further. I felt that I had got to put an end to that dreadful noise. It seemed dreadful to see the great beast lying there, powerless to move and yet powerless to die, and not even to be able to finish him. I sent back for my small rifle and poured shot after shot into his heart and down his throat. 5 They seemed to make no impression. The tortured gasps continued as steadily as the ticking of a clock.

In the end I could not stand it any longer and went away. I heard later that it took him half an hour to die. Burmans were bringing dahs and baskets even before I left, and I was told they had stripped his 10 body almost to the bones by the afternoon.

Afterwards, of course, there were endless discussions about the shooting of the elephant. The owner was furious, but he was only an Indian and could do nothing. Besides, legally I had done the right thing, for a mad elephant has to be killed, like a mad dog, if its owner 15 fails to control it. Among the Europeans opinion was divided. The older men said I was right, the younger men said it was a damn shame to shoot an elephant for killing a coolie, because an elephant was worth more than any damn Coringhee coolie. And afterwards I was very glad that the coolie had been killed; it put me legally in the 20 right and it gave me a sufficient pretext for shooting the elephant. I often wondered whether any of the others grasped that I had done it solely to avoid looking a fool.

didn't want to look like a fool (only reason he did it)

The Embassy of Cambodia

by Zadie Smith (2013)

embassy ['embəsɪ] *Botschaft*

0 – 1

Who would expect the Embassy of Cambodia? Nobody. Nobody could have expected it, or be expecting it. It's a surprise, to us all. The Embassy of Cambodia!

Next door to the embassy is a health centre. On the other side, a
5 row of private residences, most of them belonging to wealthy Arabs (or so we, the people of Willesden, contend). They have Corinthian pillars on either side of their front doors, and – it's widely believed – swimming pools out back. The embassy, by contrast, is not very grand. It is only a four- or five-bedroom North London suburban
10 villa, built at some point in the thirties, surrounded by a red brick wall, about eight feet high. And back and forth, cresting this wall horizontally, flies a shuttlecock. They are playing badminton in the Embassy of Cambodia. Pock, smash. Pock, smash.

The only real sign that the embassy is an embassy at all is the little
15 brass plaque on the door (which reads, "*THE EMBASSY OF CAMBO-DIA*") and the national flag of Cambodia (we assume that's what it is – what else could it be?) flying from the red tiled roof. Some say, "Oh, but it has a high wall around it, and this is what signifies that it is not a private residence, like the other houses on the street, but rather
20 an embassy." The people who say so are foolish. Many of the private houses have high walls, quite as high as the Embassy of Cambodia's – but they are not embassies.

residence building in which people live
Willesden area in north-west London
to **contend** (*formal*) to claim
Corinthian pillars thin columns (*Säulen*) as in ancient Greek buildings
grand impressive
thirties 1930s • **brick** *Ziegelstein*
foot/feet 1 foot = 30.48 cm
to **crest** to reach a high point and then fall
shuttlecock *Federball*
pock, smash sounds the shuttlecock makes when it is hit
brass *Messing*
plaque [plæk] *Tafel*

tiled with tiles (*Dachziegel*)
to **signify** (*formal*) to mean

foolish stupid

0 – 2

On the sixth of August, Fatou walked past the embassy for the first time, on her way to a swimming pool. It is a large pool, although not quite Olympic size. To swim a mile you must complete eighty-two lengths, which, in its very tedium, often feels as much a mental ex-
5 ercise as a physical one. The water is kept unusually warm, to please the majority of people who patronize the health centre, the kind who come not so much to swim as to lounge poolside or rest their bodies in the sauna. Fatou has swum here five or six times now, and she is often the youngest person in the pool by several decades. Gener-
10 ally, the clientele are white, or else South Asian or from the Middle East, but now and then Fatou finds herself in the water with fellow-Africans. When she spots these big men, paddling frantically like babies, struggling simply to stay afloat, she prides herself on her own abilities, having taught herself to swim, several years earlier, at the
15 Carib Beach Resort, in Accra. Not in the hotel pool – no employees were allowed in the pool. No, she learned by struggling through the rough grey sea, on the other side of the resort walls. Rising and sinking, rising and sinking, on the dirty foam. No tourist ever stepped

Fatou [fæ'tuː]

mile 1 mile = 1.609 km
tedium ['tiːdɪəm] boredom

to **patronize** *here:* to go somewhere as a regular customer
to **lounge** [laʊndʒ] to sit or lie somewhere in a relaxed way
decade ['dekeɪd] *Jahrzehnt*
clientele [ˌkliːənˈtel] *Kundschaft*
fellow- *Mit-*
to **spot** to suddenly notice
to **paddle** *planschen*
afloat on the surface

Accra capital of Ghana

rough [rʌf] *here:* with large and dangerous waves
foam *Schaum*

treacherous ['tretʃərəs] very dangerous
chambermaid ['tʃeɪmbəmeɪd] woman who cleans hotel rooms
reckless careless
tranquil peaceful

to **float** here: to move slowly in air
arc curve • to **smash** to hit violently

to **retrieve** here: to return successfully
to **transform** to change sth into sth else

in our midst here: in the middle of our community

ode lyric poem with great emotion

prosaic [prə'zeɪɪk] ordinary
genocide the Communist Khmer Rouge regime of Cambodia killed about 2 million people from 1975 to 1979

to **become attuned to** sth sich an etw gewöhnen
to **grunt** grunzen
The Triumph of the Will name of a 1935 Nazi propaganda film directed by Leni Riefenstahl
paved gepflastert
alternately happening by turns
under way going on at this moment
motion movement
alternately abwechselnd
to **lob** to hit in a high arc

Derawal South Asian family name
pass document that shows you have the right to enter sth

Eltham district of south-east London
counter Ladentheke
Kensal Rise area in north-west London
drawer Schublade • **faux** [fəʊ] not original
Louis XVI in the style of the time of King Louis XVI (1754-1793) of France
console ['kɒnsəʊl] a small piece of furniture
stockpile here: large number

onto the beach (it was covered with trash), much less into the cold and treacherous sea. Nor did any of the other chambermaids. Only some reckless teen-age boys, late at night, and Fatou, early in the morning. There is almost no way to compare swimming at Carib Beach and swimming in the health centre, warm as it is, tranquil as a bath. And, as Fatou passes the Embassy of Cambodia, on her way to the pool, over the high wall she sees a shuttlecock, passed back and forth between two unseen players. The shuttlecock floats in a wide arc softly rightward, and is smashed back, and this happens again and again, the first player always somehow able to retrieve the smash and transform it, once more, into a gentle, floating arc. High above, the sun tries to force its way through a cloud ceiling, grey and filled with water. Pock, smash. Pock, smash.

0 – 3

When the Embassy of Cambodia first appeared in our midst, a few years ago, some of us said, "Well, if we were poets perhaps we could have written some sort of an ode about this surprising appearance of the embassy." (For embassies are usually to be found in the centre of the city. This was the first one we had seen in the suburbs.) But we are not really a poetic people. We are from Willesden. Our minds tend toward the prosaic. I doubt there is a man or woman among us, for example, who – upon passing the Embassy of Cambodia for the first time – did not immediately think: "genocide".

0 – 4

Pock, smash. Pock, smash. This summer we watched the Olympics, becoming well attuned to grunting, and to the many other human sounds associated with effort and the triumph of the will. But the players in the garden of the Embassy of Cambodia are silent. (We can't say for sure that it is a garden – we have a limited view over the wall. It may well be a paved area, reserved for badminton.) The only sign that a game of badminton is under way at all is the motion of the shuttlecock itself, alternately being lobbed and smashed, lobbed and smashed, and always at the hour that Fatou passes on her way to the health centre to swim (just after ten in the morning on Mondays). It should be explained that it is Fatou's employers – and not Fatou – who are the true members of this health club; they have no idea that she uses their guest passes in this way. (Mr and Mrs Derawal and their three children – aged seventeen, fifteen, and ten – live on the same street as the embassy, but the road is almost a mile long, with the embassy at one end and the Derawals at the other.) Fatou's deception is possible only because on Mondays Mr Derawal drives to Eltham to visit his mini-market there, and Mrs Derawal works the counter in the family's second mini-mart, in Kensal Rise. In the slim drawer of a faux-Louis XVI console, in the entrance hall of the Derawals' primary residence, one can find a stockpile of guest passes. Nobody besides Fatou seems to remember that they are there.

Since August 6th (the first occasion on which she noticed the badminton), Fatou has made a point of pausing by the bus stop opposite the embassy for five or ten minutes before she goes in to swim, idle minutes she can hardly afford (Mrs Derawal returns to the house at
5 lunchtime) and yet seems unable to forgo. Such is the strangely compelling aura of the embassy. Usually, Fatou gains nothing from this waiting and observing, but on a few occasions she has seen people arrive at the embassy and watched as they are buzzed through the gate. Young white people carrying rucksacks. Often they are scruffy,
10 and wearing sandals, despite the cool weather. None of the visitors so far have been visibly Cambodian. These young people are likely looking for visas. They are buzzed in and then pass through the gate, although Fatou would really have to stand on top of the bus stop to get a view of whoever it is that lets them in. What she can say with
15 certainty is that these occasional arrivals have absolutely no effect on the badminton, which continues in its steady pattern, first gentle, then fast, first soft and high, then hard and low.

idle [ˈaɪdl] lazy, unproductive

to **forgo** to do without
compelling fascinating

buzzed through the gate *here:* allowed to
go through the gate after the buzzer is
activated
scruffy *(informal)* shabby
visibly from one's appearance

pattern *Muster*

0 – 5

On the twentieth of August, long after the Olympians had returned to their respective countries, Fatou noticed that a basketball hoop had appeared in the far corner of the garden, its net of synthetic white rope rising high enough to be seen over the wall. But no basketball
5 was ever played – at least not when Fatou was passing. The following week it had been moved closer to Fatou's side of the wall. (It must be a mobile hoop, on casters.) Fatou waited a week, two weeks, but still no basketball game replaced the badminton, which carried on as before.

respective *jeweilig*
hoop ring though which basketball players
try to throw the ball

casters small wheels

0 – 6

When I say that we were surprised by the appearance of the Embassy of Cambodia, I don't mean to suggest that the embassy is in any way unique in its peculiarity. In fact, this long, wide street is notable for a number of curious buildings, in the context of which the Embassy of
5 Cambodia does not seem especially strange. There is a mansion called GARYLAND, with something else in Arabic engraved below GARYLAND, and both the English and the Arabic text are inlaid in pink-and-green marble pillars that bookend a gigantic fence, far higher than the embassy's, better suited to a fortress. Dramatic golden gates
10 open automatically to let vehicles in and out. At any one time, GARYLAND has five to seven cars parked in its driveway.

There is a house with a huge pink elephant on the doorstep, apparently made of mosaic tiles.

There is a Catholic nunnery with a single red Ford Focus parked
15 in front. There is a Sikh institute. There is a faux-Tudor house with a pool that Mickey Rooney rented for a season, while he was performing in the West End fifteen summers ago. That house sits opposite a dingy retirement home, where one sometimes sees distressed souls,

peculiarity unusual characteristic
notable striking
curious *here:* unusual
mansion [ˈmænʃn] large, imposing house
engraved *eingraviert*
inlaid set in the surface
marble *Marmor*
to **bookend** to be at either side of sth
fortress *Burg*
vehicle [ˈviːəkl] *(formal)* car, truck, bus
tile *Fliese*
nunnery *Nonnenkloster*

Sikh [siːk] small religious group in India
Tudor in the style of the age of the Tudor
kings and queens (15th/16th century)
Mickey Rooney (1920-2014) American actor
West End London theatre district
dingy [ˈdɪndʒi] dark and dirty
retirement home home for elderly people
distressed upset and anxious

barely only just
dressing gown *Bademantel*
chestnut *Kastanie*
Brondesbury area in north-west London
    with British, Irish, Jewish, Black and
    South Asian communities

to **discard** *(formal)* to get rid of sth
Metro name of a free newspaper
brief short
to **confirm** *bestätigen*

Ivory Coast country in west Africa
employment work

Libya country in north Africa
sacrifice *Opfer*
paper newspaper
tribe *Stamm*
to **slap** to hit with the open hand

passport document one needs to travel
    abroad
wages money you earn for work
to **retain** *(formal)* to keep

to **be confined to** to be forced to stay in a
    certain area
Oyster Card plastic card used for payment
    for public transport in London
change money that is left when one buys
    sth
receipt [rɪˈsiːt] *Beleg, Quittung*

premises *(only pl)* building

to **worship** to attend a church service
just off near

guard *Wächter*
the City financial district in central London
semi half
Mass [mæs] *Messe*
to **disguise** [dɪsˈgaɪz] to hide
sturdy strong, robust
bra *BH* · **plain** simple
knickers *Damenschlüpfer*

barely covered by their dressing gowns, standing on their tiny balconies, staring into the tops of the chestnut trees.

So we are hardly strangers to curious buildings, here in Willesden & Brondesbury. And yet still we find the Embassy of Cambodia a little surprising. It is not the right sort of surprise, somehow.   5

0 – 7

In a discarded *Metro* found on the floor of the Derawal kitchen, Fatou read with interest a story about a Sudanese "slave" living in a rich man's house in London. It was not the first time that Fatou had wondered if she herself was a slave, but this story, brief as it was, confirmed in her own mind that she was not. After all, it was her father, and not 5 a kidnapper, who had taken her from Ivory Coast to Ghana, and when they reached Accra they had both found employment in the same hotel. Two years later, when she was eighteen, it was her father again who had organized her difficult passage to Libya and then on to Italy – a not insignificant financial sacrifice on his part. Also, Fatou could 10 read English – and speak a little Italian – and this girl in the paper could not read or speak anything except the language of her tribe. And nobody beat Fatou, although Mrs Derawal had twice slapped her in the face, and the two older children spoke to her with no respect at all and thanked her for nothing. (Sometimes she heard her name used as 15 a term of abuse between them. "You're as black as Fatou." Or "You're as stupid as Fatou.") On the other hand, just like the girl in the newspaper, she had not seen her passport with her own eyes since she arrived at the Derawals', and she had been told from the start that her wages were to be retained by the Derawals to pay for the food and water and 20 heat she would require during her stay, as well as to cover the rent for the room she slept in. In the final analysis, however, Fatou was not confined to the house. She had an Oyster Card, given to her by the Derawals, and was trusted to do the food shopping and other outside tasks for which she was given cash and told to return with change and receipts 25 for everything. If she did not go out in the evenings that was only because she had no money with which to go out, and anyway knew very few people in London. Whereas the girl in the paper was not allowed to leave her employers' premises, not ever – she was a prisoner.

On Sunday mornings, for example, Fatou regularly left the house 30 to meet her church friend Andrew Okonkwo at the 98 bus stop and go with him to worship at the Sacred Heart of Jesus, just off the Kilburn High Road. Afterwards Andrew always took her to a Tunisian café, where they had coffee and cake, which Andrew, who worked as a night guard in the City, always paid for. And on Mondays Fatou 35 swam. In very warm water, and thankful for the semi-darkness in which the health club, for some reason, kept its clientele, as if the place were a night club, or a midnight Mass. The darkness helped disguise the fact that her swimming costume was in fact a sturdy black bra and a pair of plain black cotton knickers. No, on balance she did 40 not think she was a slave.

0 – 8

The woman exiting the Embassy of Cambodia did not look especially like a New Person or an Old Person – neither clearly of the city nor of the country – and of course it is a long time since this division meant anything in Cambodia. Nor did these terms mean anything to
5 Fatou, who was curious only to catch her first sighting of a possible Cambodian anywhere near the Embassy of Cambodia. She was particularly interested in the woman's clothes, which were precise and utilitarian – a grey shirt tucked tightly into a pair of tan slacks, a blue mackintosh, a droopy rain hat – just as if she were a man, or no dif-
10 ferent from a man. Her straight black hair was cut short. She had in her hands many bags from Sainsbury's, and this Fatou found a little mysterious: where was she taking all that shopping? It also surprised her that the woman from the Embassy of Cambodia should shop in the same Willesden branch of Sainsbury's where Fatou shopped for
15 the Derawals. She had an idea that Oriental people had their own, secret establishments. (She believed the Jews did, too.) She both admired and slightly resented this self-reliance, but had no doubt that it was the secret to holding great power, as a people. For example, when the Chinese had come to Fatou's village to take over the mine,
20 an abiding local mystery had been: what did they eat and where did they eat it? They certainly did not buy food in the market, or from the Lebanese traders along the main road. They made their own arrangements. (Whether back home or here, the key to surviving as a people, in Fatou's opinion, was to make your own arrangements.)
25 But, looking again at the bags the Cambodian woman carried, Fatou wondered whether they weren't in fact very old bags – hadn't their design changed? The more she looked at them the more convinced she became that they contained not food but clothes or something else again, the outline of each bag being a little too rounded and
30 smooth. Maybe she was simply taking out the rubbish. Fatou stood at the bus stop and watched until the Cambodian woman reached the corner, crossed, and turned left toward the high road. Meanwhile, back at the embassy the badminton continued to be played, though with a little more effort now because of a wayward wind. At one
35 point it seemed to Fatou that the next lob would blow southward, sending the shuttlecock over the wall to land lightly in her own hands. Instead the other player, with his vicious reliability (Fatou had long ago decided that both players were men), caught the shuttlecock as it began to drift and sent it back to his opponent – another deathly,
40 downward smash.

0 – 9

No doubt there are those who will be critical of the narrow, essentially local scope of Fatou's interest in the Cambodian woman from the Embassy of Cambodia, but we, the people of Willesden, have some sympathy with her attitude. The fact is if we followed the history of
5 every little country in this world – in its dramatic as well as its quiet

---

on balance all in all
New/Old Person The Khmer Rouge wanted to radically change Cambodia into an agrarian society. Cities were to be destroyed. In their ideology, a New Person was sb who lived in the city and was educated, an Old Person was a member of the new agrarian society.
division separation
sighting seeing sb/sth
utilitarian *(formal)* designed to be useful and practical
to **tuck** to push or fold into a small space
tan yellowish brown • **slacks** trousers
mackintosh waterproof raincoat
droopy hanging down
Sainsbury's chain of supermarkets
branch *Filiale*
establishment institution, business
slightly a bit
to **resent** to feel bitter or angry about sth
self-reliance [ˌself rɪˈlaɪəns] only making use of your own abilities and efforts
the Chinese In the last few decades, China has invested a lot in exploiting the natural resources of Africa.
abiding [əˈbaɪdɪŋ] *(formal)* lasting for a long time
trader sb who sells things
Lebanese traders Lebanese immigrants first came to west Africa in the mid-19th century as traders and became increasingly important in the 19th and 20th centuries.

outline *Umriss*

wayward *(formal)* difficult to control

vicious [ˈvɪʃəs] cruel and brutal

to **drift** to be carried along slowly

essentially basically
scope extent, range

times – we would have no space left in which to live our own lives or to apply ourselves to our necessary tasks, never mind indulge in occasional pleasures, like swimming. Surely there is something to be said for drawing a circle around our attention and remaining within that circle. But how large should this circle be?   5

0 – 10

It was the Sunday after Fatou saw the Cambodian that she decided to put a version of this question to Andrew, as they sat in the Tunisian café eating two large fingers of dough stuffed with cream and custard and topped with a strip of chocolate icing. Specifically, she began a conversation with Andrew about the Holocaust, as Andrew was the 5 only person she had found in London with whom she could have these deep conversations, partly because he was patient and sympathetic to her, but also because he was an educated person, currently studying for a part-time business degree at the College of North West London. With his student card he had been given free, twenty-four- 10 hour access to the Internet.

"But more people died in Rwanda," Fatou argued. "And nobody speaks about that! Nobody!"

"Yes, I think that's true," Andrew conceded, and put the first of four sugars in his coffee. "I have to check. But, yes, millions and millions. 15 They hide the true numbers, but you can see them online. There's always a lot of hiding; it's the same all over. It's like this bureaucratic Nigerian government – they are the greatest at numerology, hiding figures, changing them to suit their purposes. I have a name for it: I call it 'demonology'. Not 'numerology' – 'demonology'. "   20

"Yes, but what I am saying is like this," Fatou pressed, wary of the conversation's drifting back, as it usually did, to the financial corruption of the Nigerian government. "Are we born to suffer? Sometimes I think we were born to suffer more than all the rest."

Andrew pushed his professorial glasses up his nose. "But, Fatou, 25 you're forgetting the most important thing. Who cried most for Jesus? His mother. Who cries most for you? Your father. It's very logical, when you break it down. The Jews cry for the Jews. The Russians cry for the Russians. We cry for Africa, because we are Africans, and, even then, I'm sorry, Fatou" – Andrew's chubby face creased up in a 30 smile – "if Nigeria plays Ivory Coast and we beat you into the ground, I'm laughing, man! I can't lie. I'm celebrating. Stomp! Stomp!" He did a little dance with his upper body, and Fatou tried, not for the first time, to imagine what he might be like as a husband, but could see only herself as the wife, and Andrew as a teenage son of hers, bright 40 and helpful, to be sure, but a son all the same – though in reality he was three years older than she. Surely it was wrong to find his baby fat and struggling mustache so off-putting. Here was a good man! She knew that he cared for her, was clean, and had given his life to Christ. Still, some part of her rebelled against him, some unholy 45 part.

---

to **apply yourself to** to work hard at
never mind erst recht nicht
to indulge in sth: to allow yourself to do sth you like

finger narrow, long shape
dough [dəʊ] Teig • **stuffed with** filled with
cream Sahne
custard yellow sauce made from eggs, sugar, milk, and flour
strip Streifen • **icing** Zuckerguss

degree Abschluss

Rwanda In this east African country, between 500,000 and 1 million people, mainly members of the Tutsi ethnic group, were killed by members of the Hutu ethnic group from April through July 1994.
to **concede** [kənˈsiːd] to admit that sth is true

to **press** here: to insist
wary [ˈweri] cautious, watchful

to **break** sth **down** to analyse the component parts of sth
chubby somewhat fat
to **crease up** to form a line in the skin
to beat sb **into the ground** to completely defeat sb

bright intelligent

mustache [məˈstɑːʃ] line of hair on the upper lip
off-putting (informal, BE) unattractive
unholy unheilig

"Hush your mouth," she said, trying to sound more playful than disgusted, and was relieved when he stopped jiggling and laid both his hands on the table, his face suddenly quite solemn.

"Believe me, that's a natural law, Fatou, pure and simple. Only God
5 cries for us all, because we are *all* his children. It's very, very logical. You just have to think about it for a moment."

Fatou sighed, and spooned some coffee foam into her mouth. "But I still think we have more pain. I've seen it myself. Chinese people have never been slaves. They are always protected from the worst."

10 Andrew took off his glasses and rubbed them on the end of his shirt. Fatou could tell that he was preparing to lay knowledge upon her.

"Fatou, think about it for a moment, please: what about Hiroshima?"

15 It was a name Fatou had heard before, but sometimes Andrew's superior knowledge made her nervous. She would find herself struggling to remember even the things she had believed she already knew.

"The big wave ..." she began, uncertainly – it was the wrong answer. He laughed mightily and shook his head at her.

20 "No, man! Big bomb. Biggest bomb in the world, made by the U.S.A., of course. They killed five million people in *one second*. Can you imagine that? You think just because your eyes are like this" he tugged the skin at both temples – "you're always protected? Think again. This bomb, even if it didn't blow you up, a week later it melted
25 the skin off your bones."

Fatou realized that she had heard this story before, or some version of it. But she felt the same vague impatience with it as she did with all accounts of suffering in the distant past. For what could be done about the suffering of the past?

30 "OK," she said. "Maybe all people have their hard times, in the past of history, but I still say –"

"Here is a counterpoint," Andrew said, reaching out and gripping her shoulder. "Let me ask you, Fatou, seriously, think about this. I'm sorry to interrupt you, but I have thought a lot about this and I want
35 to pass it on to you, because I know you care about things seriously, not like these people." He waved a hand at the assortment of cake eaters at other tables. "You're not like the other girls I know, just thinking about the club and their hair. You're a person who thinks. I told you before, anything you want to know about, ask me – I'll look it up,
40 I'll do the research. I have access. Then I'll bring it to you."

"You're a very good friend to me, Andrew, I know that."

"Listen, we are friends to each other. In this world you need friends. But, Fatou, listen to my question. It's a counterpoint to what you have been saying. Tell me, why would God choose us especially
45 for suffering when we, above all others, praise his name? Africa is the fastest-growing Christian continent! Just think about it for a minute! It doesn't even make sense!"

---

hush your mouth be quiet
to **jiggle** to move quickly side to side and up and down
solemn serious

to **sigh** [saɪ] *seufzen*

Hiroshima Japanese city destroyed by an American atomic bomb on 6 August 1945, which killed between 90,000 and 166,000 people before the end of the year
superior much more extensive

to **tug** to pull hard · **temple** *Schläfe*

bone *Knochen*

impatience *Ungeduld*
account description of an event

counterpoint contrasting element
to grip to take hold of

assortment collection, variety

devil *Teufel*

the Overground suburban rail network
   serving London and its surrounding area
clammy *feucht, klamm*
high-smelling smelling very much
Acton Central railway station in the west
   of London
bed-sit *(BE)* room rented to sleep and live in
on her account because of her

plait [plæt] *Zopf*
bun *Haarknoten, Dutt*

chastely in a manner not showing or
   expressing sexual feelings
to **linger** to continue longer than expected

to **get changed** to put on new clothes
to **rush** to move quickly
lamb [læm] meat of a young sheep
pointless not worth doing
wicker basket *Weidenkorb*
master bedroom main bedroom
to **blare** to make a loud, unpleasant sound
to **head for** to move in the direction of
laundry bin container for dirty clothes
lid cover

trout fish *Forelle*
to **punch** to hit hard with your fist
to **stoop** to bend down
to **retrieve** sth *(formal)* to get sth back
strike act of hitting or kicking
frantic hectic
throat the inside of the neck
prayer *Gebet*
to **bulge** to stick out
to **veer** to change direction

waist *Taille*
marble small round glass ball
iridescent bright • **ribbon** narrow strip

"But it's not him," Fatou said quietly, looking over Andrew's shoulder at the rain beating on the window. "It's the Devil."

0 – 11

Andrew and Fatou sat in the Tunisian coffee shop, waiting for it to stop raining, but it did not stop raining, and at three pm Fatou said she would just have to get wet. She shared Andrew's umbrella as far as the Overground, letting him pull her into his clammy, high-smelling body as they walked. At Brondesbury station Andrew had to 5 get the train, and so they said goodbye. Several times he tried to press his umbrella on her, but Fatou knew the walk from Acton Central to Andrew's bed-sit was long and she refused to let him suffer on her account.

"Big woman. Won't let anybody protect you." 10

"Rain doesn't scare me."

Fatou took from her pocket a swimming cap she had found on the floor of the health-club changing room. She wound her plaits into a bun and pulled the cap over her head.

"That's a very original idea," Andrew said, laughing. "You should 15 market that! Make your first million!"

"Peace be with you," Fatou said, and kissed him chastely on the cheek. Andrew did the same, lingering a little longer with his kiss than was necessary.

0 – 12

By the time Fatou reached the Derawals', only her hair was dry, but before going to get changed she rushed to the kitchen to take the lamb out of the freezer, though it was pointless – there were not enough hours before dinner – and then upstairs to collect the dirty clothes from the matching wicker baskets in four different bedrooms. 5 There was no one in the master bedroom, or in Faizul's, or Julie's. Downstairs a television was blaring. Entering Asma's room, hearing nothing, assuming it empty, Fatou headed straight for the laundry bin in the corner. As she opened the lid she felt a hand hit her hard on the back; she turned around. 10

There was the youngest, Asma, in front of her, her mouth open like a trout fish. Before Fatou could understand, Asma punched the huge pile of clothes out of her hands. Fatou stooped to retrieve them. While she was kneeling on the floor, another strike came, a kick to her arm. She left the clothes where they were and got up, frightened 15 by her own anger. But when she looked at Asma now she saw the girl gesturing frantically at her own throat, then putting her hands together in prayer, and then back to her throat once more. Her eyes were bulging. She veered suddenly to the right; she threw herself over the back of a chair. When she turned back to Fatou her face was 20 grey and Fatou understood finally and ran to her, grabbed her round her waist, and pulled upward as she had been taught in the hotel. A marble – with an iridescent ribbon of blue at its centre, like a wave – flew from the child's mouth and landed wetly in the carpet's plush.

Asma wept and drew in frantic gulps of air. Fatou gave her a hug, and worried when the clothes would get done. Together they went
5 down to the den, where the rest of the family was watching "Britain's Got Talent" on a flat-screen TV attached to the wall. Everybody stood at the sight of Asma's wild weeping. Mr Derawal paused the Sky box. Fatou explained about the marble.

"How many times I tell you not to put things in your mouth?" Mr
10 Derawal asked, and Mrs Derawal said something in their language – Fatou heard the name of their God – and pulled Asma onto the sofa and stroked her daughter's silky black hair.

"I couldn't breathe, man! I couldn't call nobody," Asma cried. "I was gonna die!"

15 "What you putting marbles in your mouth for anyway, you idiot," Faizul said, and un-paused the Sky box. "What kind of chief puts a marble in her mouth? Idiot. Bet you was bricking it."

"Oi, she saved your life," said Julie, the eldest child, whom Fatou generally liked the least. "Fatou saved your life. That's deep."

20 "I woulda just done this," Faizul said, and performed an especially dramatic Heimlich to his own skinny body. "And if that didn't work I woulda just start pounding myself karate style, bam bam bam bam bam –"

"Faizul!" Mr Derawal shouted, and then turned stiffly to Fatou,
25 and spoke not to her, exactly, but to a point somewhere between her elbow and the sunburst mirror behind her head. "Thank you, Fatou. It's lucky you were there."

Fatou nodded and moved to leave, but at the doorway to the den Mrs Derawal asked her if the lamb had defrosted and Fatou had to
30 confess that she had only just taken it out. Mrs Derawal said something sharply in her language. Fatou waited for something further, but Mr Derawal only smiled awkwardly at her, and nodded as a sign that she could go now. Fatou went upstairs to collect the clothes.

0 – 13

"To keep you is no benefit. To destroy you is no loss" was one of the mottoes of the Khmer Rouge. It referred to the New People, those city dwellers who could not be made to give up city life and work on a farm. By returning everybody to the land, the regime hoped to create
5 a society of Old People – that is to say, of agrarian peasants. When a New Person was relocated from the city to the country, it was vital not to show weakness in the fields. Vulnerability was punishable by death.

In Willesden, we are almost all New People, though some of us,
10 like Fatou, were, until quite recently, Old People, working the land in our various countries of origin. Of the Old and New People of Willesden I speak; I have been chosen to speak for them, though they did not choose me and must wonder what gives me the right. I could

---

plush thick, costly surface
frantic hectic
gulps of air deep breaths
hug act of putting your arms around sb
den room in a house where people can relax, watch TV, etc.
Britain's Got Talent talent show on British TV
attached fixed
to **pause/un-pause** to stop the TV/start it again
Sky box TV receiver sold by Sky, a pay TV company
to **weep** to cry
to **stroke** sth: to move your hand gently over sth
gonna (slang) going to

chief (London slang) spastic
to brick it (vulgar) vor Angst in die Hose machen
oi (BE) Hey!
deep (informal) quite amazing
woulda (slang) would have
Heimlich first aid procedure to remove objects from sb's throat
skinny thin · to **pound** to hit hard

stiffly steif

sunburst mirror mirror surrounded by a design looking like the rays of the sun

to **nod** nicken
to **defrost** auftauen

to **confess** to admit

awkwardly in a manner showing you are embarrassed

benefit advantage · **loss** Verlust

dweller sb who lives somewhere
agragrian connected with farming

peasant ['peznt] simple farmer

to **relocate** to move sb somewhere else
vulnerability quality of being weak or easily hurt

crossroads place where two or more roads meet
Kilburn, Queen's Park areas in north-west London
swift quick • **damning** very critical
overlooking with a view to

gormless (BE) stupid

delivered the smashes hit the shuttlecock hard
clumsy unbeholfen
crawl Kraulen
dimly lit dark
snapper a kind of fish
deck area for sitting outside
bow tie Fliege
askew [əˈskjuː] with one side lower than the other
lap Schoß

to **hook** sth **around** sth: to put sth tightly around sth

scrawny very thin
ballroom large room for dancing

cabin small wooden house

to **crouch** to lower your body by bending your legs

congregation members of a church
to **pour out** here: to leave in great numbers
coach Reisebus • **baptism** Taufe
congregant member of a congregation
to **bloat** to swell

surface Oberfläche

say, "Because I was born at the crossroads of Willesden, Kilburn, and Queen's Park!" But the reply would be swift and damning: "Oh, don't be foolish, many people were born right there; it doesn't mean anything at all. We are not one people and no one can speak for us. It's all a lot of nonsense. We see you standing on the balcony, overlooking ⁵ the Embassy of Cambodia, in your dressing gown, staring into the chestnut trees, looking gormless. The real reason you speak in this way is because you can't think of anything better to do."

0 – 14

On Monday, Fatou went swimming. She paused to watch the badminton. She thought that the arm that delivered the smashes must make a movement similar to the one she made in the pool, with her clumsy yet effective front crawl. She entered the health centre and gave a guest pass to the girl behind the desk. In the dimly lit changing room, ⁵ she put on her sturdy black underwear. As she swam, she thought of Carib Beach. Her father serving snapper to the guests on the deck, his bow tie always a little askew, the ugly tourists, the whole scene there. Of course, it was not surprising in the least to see old white men from Germany with beautiful local girls on their laps, but she would ¹⁰ never forget the two old white women from England – red women, really, thanks to the sun – each of them as big as two women put together, with Kweku and Osai lying by their sides, the boys hooking their scrawny black bird-arms round the women's massive red shoulders, dancing with them in the hotel "ballroom", answering to ¹⁵ the names Michael and David, and disappearing into the women's cabins at night. She had known the boys' real girlfriends; they were chambermaids like Fatou. Sometimes they cleaned the rooms where Kweku and Osai spent the night with the English women. And the girls themselves had "boyfriends" among the guests. It was not a holy ²⁰ place, that hotel. And the pool was shaped like a kidney bean: nobody could really swim in it, or showed any sign of wanting to. Mostly, they stood in it and drank cocktails. Sometimes they even had their burgers delivered to the pool. Fatou hated to watch her father crouching to hand a burger to a man waist high in water. ²⁵

The only good thing that happened in Carib Beach was this: once a month, on a Sunday, the congregation of a local church poured out of a coach at the front gates, lined up fully dressed in the courtyard, and then walked into the pool for a mass baptism. The tourists were never warned, and Fatou never understood why the congregants ³⁰ were allowed to do it. But she loved to watch their white shirts bloat and spread across the surface of the water, and to hear the weeping and singing. At the time – though she was not then a member of that church, or of any church except the one in her heart – she had felt that this baptism was for her, too, and that it kept her safe, and that ³⁵ this was somehow the reason she did not become one of the "girls" at the Carib Beach Resort. For almost two years – between her father's efforts and the grace of an unseen and unacknowledged God – she did her work, and swam Sunday mornings at the crack of dawn, and got along all right. But the Devil was waiting.

5 She had only a month left in Accra when she entered a bedroom to clean it one morning and heard the door shut softly behind her before she could put a hand to it. He came, this time, in Russian form. Afterwards, he cried and begged her not to tell anyone: his wife had gone to see the Cape Coast Castle and they were leaving the following morning. Fatou listened to his blubbering and realized that he 10 thought the hotel would punish him for his action, or that the police would be called. That was when she knew that the Devil was stupid as well as evil. She spat in his face and left. Thinking about the Devil now made her swimming fast and angry, and for a while she easily lapped the young white man in the lane next to hers, the faster lane.

0 – 15

"Don't give the Devil your anger, it is his food," Andrew had said to her, when they first met, a year ago. He handed her a leaflet as she sat eating a sandwich on a bench in Kilburn Park. "Don't make it so easy for him." Without being invited, he took the seat next to hers 5 and began going through the text of his leaflet. It was printed to look like a newspaper, and he started with the headline: "*WHY IS THERE PAIN?*" She liked him. They began a theological conversation. It continued in the Tunisian café, and every Sunday for several months. A lot of the things he said she had heard before from other people, and 10 they did not succeed in changing her attitude. In the end, it was one thing that he said to her that really made the difference. It was after she'd told him this story:

"One day, at the hotel, I heard a commotion on the beach. It was early morning. I went out and I saw nine children washed up dead 15 on the beach. Ten or eleven years old, boys and girls. They had gone into the water, but they didn't know how to swim. Some people were crying, maybe two people. Everyone else just shook their heads and carried on walking to where they were going. After a long time, the police came. The bodies were taken away. People said, 'Well, they 20 are with God now.' Everybody carried on like before. I went back to work. The next year I arrived in Rome. I saw a boy who was about fifteen years old knocked down on his bike. He was dead. People were screaming and crying in the street. Everybody crying. They were not his family. They were only strangers. The next day, it was in the 25 paper."

And Andrew replied, "A tap runs fast the first time you switch it on."

0 – 16

Twenty more laps. Fatou tried to think of the last time she had cried. It was in Rome, but it wasn't for the boy on the bike. She was cleaning toilets in a Catholic girls' school. She did not know Jesus then, so it made no difference what kind of school it was – she knew only that

effort working hard to achieve sth
grace Gnade
unacknowledged not recognized, not considered to exist
crack of dawn very early in the morning
to **get along all right** to manage to live and work without any problems
to **beg** betteln, flehen
Cape Coast Castle castle in Ghana formerly used to hold slaves in dungeons before they were shipped to America
blubbering crying

to **spit, spat, spat** spucken
to **lap** to pass
lane here: narrow marked section of a swimming pool

bench what people sit on e.g. in a park

commotion sudden, noisy confusion
washed up … on the beach carried by waves onto the beach

to **carry on** to continue
body Leiche

to **knock down** to hit violently

tap (BE) Wasserhahn
to **switch on** to turn on

lap distance swum from one end of a pool to the other

speaking of her time in Rome [handwritten]

fountain ['faʊntən] *Springbrunnen*
to **spot** to notice suddenly
odd strange • **tin** metal container
spray can metal container used to spray
    e.g. paint
Statue of Liberty famous statue in New
    York harbour
identity card *Ausweis*
tub small, round container
slit long, narrow opening
stain dirty mark
envious *neidisch*
Bengali from Bengal, a region in the eastern
    part of India and in Bangladesh
Via Nazionale street in Rome, one of the
    city's main commercial centres, attracting
    many tourists
closed shop The usual meaning of "closed
    shop" is a firm whose employees are
    required to belong to one single union
    (*Gewerkschaft*).
stall small area in a room separated by
    walls
pile *Stapel*
frog *Frosch*
to **baptize** *taufen*
sin *Sünde* • to **wipe** *here:* to remove
virgin a person who has never had sex
inch 1 inch = 2.54 cm

found Smith in the bushes [handwritten]

baptized Andrew Fatou [handwritten]

she thought she would be happy forever [handwritten]

cautiously carefully

pissed off *(vulgar)* very angry
wise up *(informal)* become aware that there
    are unpleasant situations

Mrs Derawal gets offended by Fatou's question [handwritten]

fuss unnecessary worry, excitement

---

she was cleaning toilets. At midday, she had a fifteen-minute break. She would go to the little walled garden across the road to smoke a cigarette. One day, she was sitting on a bench near a fountain, and spotted something odd in the bushes. A tin of green paint. A gold spray can. A Statue of Liberty costume. An identity card with the name Rajib Devanga. One shoe. An empty wallet. A plastic tub with a slit cut in the top meant for coins and euro notes – empty. A little stain of what looked like blood on this tub. Until that point, she had been envious of the Bengali boys on Via Nazionale. She felt that she, too, could paint herself green and stand still for an hour. But when she tried to find out more the Bengalis would not talk to her. It was a closed shop, for brown men only. Her place was in the bathroom stalls. She thought those men had it easy. Then she saw that little sad pile of belongings in the bush and cried; for herself or for Rajib, she wasn't sure.

Now she turned onto her back in the water for the final two laps, relaxed her arms, and kicked her feet out like a frog. Water made her think of more water. "When you're baptized in our church, all sin is wiped, you start again": Andrew's promise. She had never told Andrew of the sin precisely, but she knew that he knew she was not a virgin. The day she finally became a Catholic, 6 February 2011, Andrew had taken her, hair still wet, to the Tunisian café and asked her how it felt.

She was joyful! She said, "I feel like a new person!"

But happiness like that is hard to hold on to. Back at work the next day, picking Julie's dirty underwear up off the floor inches from the wicker basket, she had to keep reminding herself of her new relationship with Jesus and how it changed everything. Didn't it change everything? The following Sunday she expressed some of her doubt, cautiously, to Andrew.

"But did you think you'd never feel sad again? Never angry or tired or just pissed off – sorry about my language. Come on, Fatou! Wise up, man!"

Was it wrong to hope to be happy?

0 – 17

Lost to these watery thoughts, Fatou got home a little later than usual and was through the door only minutes before Mrs Derawal.

"How is Asma?" Fatou asked. She had heard the girl cry out in the night.

"My goodness, it was just a little marble," Mrs Derawal said, and Fatou realized that it was not in her imagination: since Sunday night, neither of the adult Derawals had been able to look her in the eye. "What a fuss everybody is making. I have a list for you – it's on the table."

0 – 18

Fatou watched Andrew pick his way through the tables in the Tunisian café, holding a tray with a pair of mochas on it and some croissants. He hit the elbow of one man with his backside and then trailed
5 the belt of his long, silly leather coat through the lunch of another, apologizing as he went. You could not say that he was an elegant man. But he was generous, he was thoughtful. She stood up to push a teetering croissant back onto its plate. They sat down at the same time, and smiled at each other.

10 "A while ago you asked me about Cambodia," Andrew said. "Well, it's a very interesting case." He tapped the frame of his glasses. "If you even wore a pair of these? They would kill you. Glasses meant you thought too much. They had very primitive ideas. They were enemies of logic and progress. They wanted everybody to go back to the coun-
15 try and live like simple people."

"But sometimes it's true that things are simpler in the country."

"In some ways. I don't really know. I've never lived in the country."

I don't really know. It was good to hear him say that! It was a good sign. She smiled cheekily at him. "People are less sinful in the coun-
20 try," she said, but he did not seem to see that she was flirting with him, and embarked on another lecture:

"That's true. But you can't force people to live in the country. That's what I call a Big Man Policy. I invented this phrase for my dissertation. We know all about Big Man Policies in Nigeria. They
25 come from the top, and they crush you. There's always somebody who wants to be the Big Man, and take everything for himself, and tell everybody how to think and what to do. When, actually, it's he who is weak. But if the Big Men see that *you* see that *they* are weak they have no choice but to destroy you. That is the real tragedy."

30 Fatou sighed. "I never met a man who didn't want to tell everybody how to think and what to do," she said.

Andrew laughed. "Fatou, you include me? Are you a feminist now, too?"

Fatou brought her mug up to her lips and looked penetratingly at
35 Andrew. There were good and bad kinds of weakness in men, and she had come to the conclusion that the key was to know which kind you were dealing with.

"Andrew," she said, putting her hand on his, "would you like to come swimming with me?"

40

0 – 19

Because Fatou believed that the Derawals' neighbours had been instructed to spy on her, she would not let Andrew come to the house to pick her up on Monday, instead leaving as she always did, just be-
45 fore ten, carrying misleading Sainsbury's bags and walking towards the health centre. She spotted him from a long way off – the road was so straight and he had arrived early. He stood shivering in the drizzle. She felt sorry, but also a little prideful: it was the prospect

---

Glossary (right margin):

to **pick** one's **way** to walk carefully
tray Tablett
mocha ['mɒkə] strong, dark coffee from Arabia
to **trail** to allow to slide along behind
belt Gürtel
thoughtful aufmerksam
to **teeter** to be in an unsteady position ready to fall

to **tap** to hit lightly
frame Gestell

[handwritten note: in café talking about cambodia and now you weren't supposed to wear glasses]

cheekily (BE, informal) frech

to **embark on** sth: to start with sth new
lecture Vortrag

to **crush** to destroy by breaking into pieces

mug cup with a flat bottom
penetratingly durchdringend

to **instruct** to tell sb to do sth
to **spy** [spaɪ] **on** sb jdn bespitzeln
misleading giving you the wrong impression
from a long way off from far away
to **shiver** ['ʃɪvə(r)] to shake slightly
drizzle ['drɪz(ə)l] light rain
prospect possibility

spot *here:* place

of seeing her body that had raised this big man from his bed. Still, it was a sacrifice, she knew, for her friend to come out to meet her on a weekday morning. He worked all night long and kept the daytime for sleeping. She watched him waving at her from their agreed meeting spot, just on the corner, in front of the Embassy of Cambodia. After a while, he stopped waving – because she was still so far away – and then, a little later, he began waving again. She waved back, and when she finally reached him they surprised each other by holding hands.

to weep for mercy *um Gnade betteln*

"I'm an excellent badminton player," Andrew said, as they passed the Embassy of Cambodia. "I would make you weep for mercy! Next time, instead of swimming we should play badminton somewhere." Next time, we should go to Paris. Next time, we should go to the moon. He was a dreamer. But there are worse things, Fatou thought, than being a dreamer.

0 – 20

"So you're a guest and this is your guest?" the girl behind the desk asked.

"I am a guest and this is another guest," Fatou replied.

"Yeah ... that's not really how it works?"

"Please," Fatou said. "We've come from a long way."

to **appreciate** [əˈpriːʃieɪt] *here:* to understand, to realize

"I appreciate that," the girl said. "But I really shouldn't let you in, to be honest."

"Please," Fatou said again. She could think of no other argument.

The girl took out a pen and made a mark on Fatou's guest pass.

"This one time. Don't tell no one I did this, please. One time only!

to **cross off** to mark, to draw a line through
to **approach** [əˈprəʊtʃ] to come nearer to
to **part** to go in different directions
with lightning speed *blitzschnell*
yet but
lounger comfortable chair to lie in
to **train** one's **eyes on** to look steadily at
to **emerge** to come into view

I'll need to cross off two separate visits."

For one time only, then, Andrew and Fatou approached the changing rooms together and parted at the doors that led to the men's and the women's. In her changing room, Fatou got ready with lightning speed. Yet somehow he was already there on a lounger when she came out, eyes trained on the women's changing-room door, waiting for her to emerge.

"Man, this is the life!" he said, putting his arms behind his head.

"Are you getting in?" Fatou asked, and tried to place her hands, casually, in front of her groin.

groin *Leiste*
to **take it all in** to observe new surroundings and enjoy what one sees

"Not yet, man, I'm just taking it all in, taking it all in. You go in. I'll come in a moment."

consistent steady, even
to **angle** to turn in a certain direction

Fatou climbed down the steps and began to swim. Not elegant, not especially fast, but consistent and determined. Every now and then she would angle her head to try to see if Andrew was still on his chair, smiling to himself. After twenty laps, she swam to where he lay and put her elbows on the tiles.

"You're not coming in? It's so warm. Like a bath."

"Sure, sure," he said. "I'll try it."

to **fold** *falten*

precise exact · **bulk** large size
wobble *Schwabbeln*

As he sat up his stomach folded in on itself, and Fatou wondered whether he had spent all that time on the lounger to avoid her seeing its precise bulk and wobble. He came towards the stairs; Fatou held out a hand to him, but he pushed it away. He made his way down and stood in the shallow end, splashing water over his shoulders like a prince fanning himself, and then crouching down into it.

"It is warm! Very nice. This is the life, man! You go, swim – I'll
5 follow you."

Fatou kicked off, creating so much splash that she heard someone in the adjacent lane complain. At the wall, she turned and looked for Andrew. His method, such as it was, involved dipping deep under the water and hanging there like a hippo, then batting his arms till
10 he crested for air, and then diving down again and hanging. It was a lot of energy to expend on such a short distance, and by the time he reached the wall he was panting like a maniac. His eyes – he had no goggles – were painfully red.

"It's OK," Fatou said, trying to take his hand again. "If you let me,
15 I'll show you how." But he shrugged her off, and rubbed at his eyes.

"There's too much bloody chlorine in this pool."

"You want to leave?"

Andrew turned back to look at Fatou. His eyes were streaming. He looked, to Fatou, like a little boy trying to disguise the fact he had
20 been crying. But then he held her hand, under the water.

"No. I'm just going to take it easy right here."

"OK," Fatou said.

"You swim. You're good. You swim."

"OK," Fatou said, and set off, and found that each lap was more
25 distracted and rhythmless than the last. She was not used to being watched while she swam. Ten laps later, she suddenly stood up half-way down the lane and walked the rest of the distance to the wall.

"You want to go in the Jacuzzi?" she asked him, pointing to it. In the hot tub sat a woman dressed in a soaking tracksuit, her head
30 covered with a head scarf. A man next to the woman, perhaps her husband, stared at Fatou and said something to her. He was so hairy he was almost as covered as she was. Together they rose up out of the water and left. He was wearing the tiniest of Speedos, the kind Fatou had feared Andrew might wear, and was grateful he had not.
35 Andrew's shorts were perfectly nice, knee length, red and solid, and looked good against his skin.

"No," Andrew said. "It's great just to be here with you, watching the world go by."

0 – 21

That same evening, Fatou was fired. Not for the guest passes – the Derawals never found out how many miles Fatou had travelled on their membership. In fact, it was hard for Fatou to understand exactly why she was being fired, as Mrs Derawal herself did not seem able to
5 explain it very precisely.

"What you don't understand is that we have no need for a nanny," she said, standing in the doorway of Fatou's room – there was not really enough space in there for two people to stand without one of

---

shallow not deep
to **fan** oneself *sich Luft zufächern*

to **kick off** to start
adjacent [əˈdʒeɪsnt] next to sth
lane *Bahn*
to **dip** to go downwards
hippo *Nilpferd*
to **bat** to make quick, short movements
to **dive** to go under water
to **expend** to use up
to **pant** to breathe heavily with the mouth open
maniac [ˈmeɪniæk] crazy person
goggles *(only pl)* glasses used for swimming
to **shrug** sb **off** to push sb away
bloody *(BE, slang)* damn
chlorine [ˈklɔːriːn] *Chlor*
to **stream** *here:* to flow with continuous tears

distracted not paying attention to what you are doing because you are worried

soaking full of water
tracksuit *Trainingsanzug*
head scarf *Kopftuch*

tiny [ˈtaɪni] very small
Speedos small swimming trunks often worn for swimming sports

nanny woman who takes care of children in a home

practically very nearly

housekeeper *Haushälterin*

them being practically on the bed. "The children are grown. We need a housekeeper, one who cleans properly. These days, you care more about the children than the cleaning," Mrs Derawal added, though Fatou had never cared for the children, not even slightly. "And that is of no use to us." 5

Fatou said nothing. She was thinking that she did not have a proper suitcase and would have to take her things from Mrs Derawal's house in plastic bags.

"And so you will want to find somewhere else to live as soon as possible," Mrs Derawal said. "My husband's cousin is coming to stay 10 in this room on Friday – this Friday."

Fatou thought about that for a moment. Then she said, "Can I please use the phone for one call?"

to **inspect** to examine closely
to **flake** to fall off in a thin, small piece
doorframe *Türrahmen*

Excuse me? *here: Wie bitte? Bitte was?*

Mrs Derawal inspected a piece of wood that had flaked from the doorframe. But she nodded. 15

"And I would like to have my passport, please."

"Excuse me?"

"My passport, please."

to **twist** to turn into an unusual shape

At last Mrs Derawal looked at Fatou, right into her eyes, but her face was twisted, as if Fatou had just reached over and slapped her. 20 Anyone could see the Devil had climbed inside poor Mrs Derawal. He was lighting her up with a pure fury.

to **light up** to make bright
fury [ˈfjʊəri] extreme anger
for goodness' sake *meine Güte, um Gottes willen*

"For goodness' sake, girl, I don't have your passport! What would I want with your passport? It's probably in a drawer in the kitchen somewhere. Is that my job now, too, to look for your things?" 25

decoy [ˈdiːkɔɪ] *here: having the quality of tricking or deceiving*

Fatou was left alone. She packed her things into the decoy shopping bags she usually took to the swimming pool. While she was doing this, someone pushed her passport under the door. An hour later, she carried her bags downstairs and went directly to the phone in the hall. Faizul walked by and lifted his hand for a high-five. Fatou 30 ignored him and dialled Andrew's number. From her friend's voice she knew that she had woken him, but he was not even the slightest bit angry. He listened to all she had to say and seemed to understand, too, without her having to say so, that at this moment she could not speak freely. After she had said her part, he asked a few quick techni- 35 cal questions and then explained clearly and carefully what was to happen.

high-five raising your hand and hitting the inside of your hand against the inside of another person's hand as a sign of approval
to **dial** [ˈdaɪəl] *wählen*
not even the slightest bit not even a little bit

"It will all be OK. They need cleaners in my offices – I will ask for you. In the meantime, you come here. We'll sleep in shifts. You can trust me. I respect you, Fatou." 40

shift *Schicht*

But she did not have her Oyster Card; it was in the kitchen, on the fridge under a magnet of Florida, and she would rather die than go in there. Fine: he could meet her at 6 pm, at the Brondesbury Overground station. Fatou looked at the grandfather clock in front of her: she had four hours to kill. 45

grandfather clock *Standuhr*
to **kill time** to spend time doing nothing in particular until sth important is to be done

"Six o' clock," she repeated. She put the phone down, took the rest of the guest passes from the drawer of the Louis XVI console, and left the house.

"Weighed down a bit today," the girl at the desk of the health club said, nodding at Fatou's collection of plastic bags. Fatou held out a guest pass for a stamp and did not smile. "See you next time," this same girl said, an hour and a half later, as Fatou strode past, still
5 weighed down and still unwilling to be grateful for past favours. Gratitude was just another kind of servitude. Better to make your own arrangements.

Walking out into the cold grey, Fatou felt a sense of brightness, of being washed clean, that neither the weather nor her new circum-
10 stance could dim. Still, her limbs were weary and her hair was wet; she would probably catch a cold, waiting out here. It was only four-thirty. She put her bags on the pavement and sat down next to them, just by the bus stop opposite the Embassy of Cambodia. Buses came and went, slowing down for her and then jerking forward when they
15 realized that she had no interest in getting up and on. Many of us walked past her that afternoon, or spotted her as we rode the bus, or through the windscreens of our cars, or from our balconies. Naturally, we wondered what this girl was doing, sitting on damp pavement in the middle of the day. We worried for her. We tend to assume the
20 worst, here in Willesden. We watched her watching the shuttlecock. Pock, smash. Pock, smash. As if one player could imagine only a violent conclusion and the other only a hopeful return.

weighed down carrying a lot of heavy things
stamp *Stempel*
to stride, strode, stridden to walk with long steps
favour *Gefälligkeit*
gratitude being grateful
servitude *Knechtschaft*

circumstance situation
to **dim** to make less bright
limbs arms and legs
weary very tired
to **catch a cold** *sich erkälten*
pavement *(BE)* sidewalk *(AE)*
to **jerk forward** to suddenly move with a short, sharp movement

windscreen *(BE)* front window of a car
damp wet

conclusion *here:* end of the game
return successful hitting back of the shuttlecock

My Son the Fanatic

by Hanif Kureishi (1994)

surreptitiously [ˌsʌrəpˈtɪʃəsli] done secretly
to **rouse** oneself: to become active again
to **seek** to look for
clue sth that helps to solve a mystery
to **bewilder** to make confused
tidy *ordentlich*
tangle chaotic arrangement of things
cricket bat flat stick used to hit the ball in cricket, a British ball game
neat clean and tidy
mess chaos • **initially** [ɪˈnɪʃəli] at first
to **outgrow** sth: to no longer do sth because you have become too old for it
dustbin (BE) container for rubbish
fashionable modern, according to the latest fashion
to **part from** sb: to leave sb
to **bring up** to mention
slightly a bit

to **elicit** (formal) to cause
conclusive putting an end to sth

eccentricity strange behaviour
injustice unfair act
pitfall unsuspected difficulty
to **stumble** *stolpern*
accountant *Buchhalter*

possessions things one owns

bare empty
to **bear, bore, borne** *here:* to reveal

imperative extremely important
sympathetic understanding and compassionate

Punjabi [pʊnˈdʒɑːbi] person from Punjab, a province of eastern Pakistan that borders on the Indian state of the same name
cabby (informal) taxi driver
practical joke *Streich* • **lewd** dirty
takeaway (BE) food sold by restaurants to be taken home
balti [ˈbɔːlti] **house** restaurant that serves *balti*, a traditional Pakistani dish

turning direction

to **skip school** *schwänzen*
to **excel at** sth [ɪkˈselˌət] to do sth very well

Surreptitiously, the father began going into his son's bedroom. He would sit there for hours, rousing himself only to seek clues. What bewildered him was that Ali was getting tidier. The room, which was usually a tangle of clothes, books, cricket bats and video games, was becoming neat and ordered; spaces began appearing where before there had been only mess. Initially, Parvez had been pleased: his son was outgrowing his teenage attitudes. But one day, beside the dustbin, Parvez found a torn shopping bag that contained not only old toys but computer disks, videotapes, new books, and fashionable clothes the boy had bought a few months before. Also without explanation, Ali had parted from the English girlfriend who used to come around to the house. His old friends stopped ringing. For reasons he didn't himself understand, Parvez was unable to bring up the subject of Ali's unusual behaviour. He was aware that he had become slightly afraid of his son, who, between his silences, was developing a sharp tongue. One remark Parvez did make – "You don't play your guitar anymore" – elicited the mysterious but conclusive reply, "There are more important things to be done."

Yet Parvez felt his son's eccentricity as an injustice. He had always been aware of the pitfalls that other men's sons had stumbled into in England. It was for Ali that Parvez worked long hours; he spent a lot of money paying for Ali's education as an accountant. He had bought Ali good suits, all the books he required, and a computer. And now the boy was throwing his possessions out! The TV, video-player and stereo system followed the guitar. Soon the room was practically bare. Even the unhappy walls bore pale marks where Ali's pictures had been removed.

Parvez couldn't sleep; he went more often to the whisky bottle, even when he was at work. He realised it was imperative to discuss the matter with someone sympathetic.

Parvez had been a taxi-driver for twenty years. Half that time he'd worked for the same firm. Like him, most of the other drivers were Punjabis. They preferred to work at night, when the roads were clearer and the money better. They slept during the day, avoiding their wives. They led almost a boy's life together in the cabbies' office, playing cards and setting up practical jokes, exchanging lewd stories, eating takeaways from local *balti* houses, and discussing politics and their own problems.

Parvez had been unable to discuss the subject of Ali with his friends. He was too ashamed. And he was afraid, too, that they would blame him for the wrong turning his boy had taken, just as he had blamed other fathers whose sons began running around with bad girls, skipping school and joining gangs. For years, Parvez had boasted to the other men about how Ali excelled in cricket, swimming and football, and what an attentive scholar he was, getting As in most subjects. Was it asking too much for Ali to get a good job, marry the right girl, and start a family? Once this happened, Parvez would be happy. His dreams of doing well in England would have come true.

5 Where had he gone wrong?

One night, sitting in the taxi office on busted chairs with his two closest friends, watching a Sylvester Stallone film, Parvez broke his silence.

"I can't understand it!" he burst out. "Everything is going from his
10 room. And I can't talk to him anymore. We were not father and son – we were brothers! Where has he gone? Why is he torturing me?" And Parvez put his head in his hands.

Even as he poured out his account, the men shook their heads and gave one another knowing glances. "Tell me what is happening!"
15 he demanded. The reply was almost triumphant. They had guessed something was going wrong. Now it was clear: Ali was taking drugs and selling his possessions to pay for them. That was why his bedroom was being emptied. "What must I do, then?"

Parvez's friends instructed him to watch Ali scrupulously and to
20 be severe with him, before the boy went mad, overdosed, or murdered someone. Parvez staggered out into the early-morning air, terrified that they were right. His boy – the drug-addict killer!

To his relief, he found Bettina sitting in his car. Usually the last customers of the night were local "brasses", or prostitutes. The taxi-
25 drivers knew them well and often drove them to liaisons. At the end of the girls' night, the men would ferry them home, though sometimes they would join the cabbies for a drinking session in the office. Occasionally, the drivers would go with the girls. "A ride in exchange for a ride," it was called.

30 Bettina had known Parvez for three years. She lived outside the town and, on the long drives home, during which she sat not in the passenger seat but beside him, Parvez had talked to her about his life and hopes, just as she talked about hers. They saw each other most nights. He could talk to her about things he'd never be able to discuss
35 with his own wife. Bettina, in turn, always reported on her night's activities. He liked to know where she had been and with whom. Once, he had rescued her from a violent client, and since then they had come to care for each other.

Though Bettina had never met Ali, she heard about the boy con-
40 tinually. That night, when Parvez told Bettina that he suspected Ali was on drugs, to Parvez's relief, she judged neither him nor the boy, but said, "It's all in the eyes." They might be bloodshot; the pupils might be dilated; Ali might look tired. He could be liable to sweats, or sudden mood changes. "OK?"

45 Parvez began his vigil gratefully. Now that he knew what the problem might be, he felt better. And surely, he figured, things couldn't have gone too far?

---

scholar excellent student

busted (AE, informal) broken
Sylvester Stallone American actor, famous for his *Rocky* and *Rambo* films

to **burst out** to suddenly speak

to **torture** *quälen*

to **pour out** *here:* to finally talk about
account description of what happened
glance quick look

scrupulously very carefully
severe strict
to **overdose** to take too much of a drug
to **stagger** to walk unsteadily as if about to fall
drug addict person who can't stop taking a drug
liaison [li'eɪʒn] *here:* meeting with a client for sex
to **ferry** to take sb somewhere frequently

for a ride i.e. for sex

had come had started

to **suspect** *vermuten*

bloodshot *blutunterlaufen* • **pupil** *Pupille*
dilated [daɪ'leɪtɪd] wider than normal
liable to sweats likely to have moments of sweating
vigil ['vɪdʒɪl] carefully watching sb/sth
to **figure** *here:* to think

drawer Schublade
to sniff here: to breathe in to identify the
  smell of sth
to inspect to examine carefully
to probe herumtasten
capsule Arzneikapsel
syringe [sɪˈrɪndʒ] Spritze
rock (slang) crack
to witness here: to observe
to flinch to draw back suddenly because of
  pain, shock, or surprise
gaze fixed look, stare • **alert** aufgeweckt
sullen bad-tempered
reproach blame

beard [bɪə(r)d] hair on the face

to resemble to be similar to
belongings possessions
to donate spenden
charity shop shop that sells used clothes,
  furniture, etc. to people in need
alarm clock Wecker
to sew [səʊ] nähen

crack narrow opening
to mutter [ˈmʌtə] murmeln
puzzled confused
clue [kluː] some information that helps to
  solve a mystery
to establish here: to determine
to pray beten • **without fail** always
Lahore [ləˈhɔː] capital of the Punjab
  province in Pakistan
maulvi [ˈmɔːlvɪ] title of a respected Muslim
  scholar
to attach anbringen • **string** Schnur
instantly immediately
to jerk to make a sudden movement
indignity Demütigung
mullah [ˈmʊlə] Muslim scholar, teacher,
  religious leader
to rove over to wander about because of
  sexual interest
inquisitive [ɪnˈkwɪzətɪv] really wanting to
  know sth
oddly strangely • **devotion** passion

He watched each mouthful the boy took. He sat beside him at every opportunity and looked into his eyes. When he could, he took the boy's hand, checked his temperature. If the boy wasn't at home, Parvez was active, looking under the carpet, in Ali's drawers, and behind the empty wardrobe – sniffing, inspecting, probing. He knew 5 what to look for: Bettina had drawn pictures of capsules, syringes, pills, powders, rocks. Every night, she waited to hear news of what he'd witnessed. After a few days of constant observation, Parvez was able to report that although the boy had given up sports, he seemed healthy. His eyes were clear. He didn't – as Parvez expected he might 10 – flinch guiltily from his father's gaze. In fact, the boy seemed more alert and steady than usual: as well as being sullen, he was very watchful. He returned his father's long looks with more than a hint of criticism, of reproach even – so much so that Parvez began to feel that it was he who was in the wrong, and not the boy. 15

"And there's nothing else physically different?" Bettina asked.

"No!" Parvez thought for a moment. "But he is growing a beard."

One night, after sitting with Bettina in an all-night coffee shop, Parvez came home particularly late. Reluctantly, he and Bettina had abandoned the drug theory, for Parvez had found nothing resembling 20 any drug in Ali's room. Besides, Ali wasn't selling his belongings. He threw them out, gave them away, or donated them to charity shops.

Standing in the hall, Parvez heard the boy's alarm clock go off. Parvez hurried into his bedroom, where his wife, still awake, was sewing in bed. He ordered her to sit down and keep quiet, though she 25 had neither stood up nor said a word. As she watched him curiously, he observed his son through the crack of the door. The boy went into the bathroom to wash. When he returned to his room, Parvez sprang across the hall and set his ear to Ali's door. A muttering sound came from within. Parvez was puzzled but relieved. 30

Once this clue had been established, Parvez watched him at other times. The boy was praying. Without fail, when he was at home, he prayed five times a day. Parvez had grown up in Lahore, where all young boys had been taught the Koran. To stop Parvez from falling asleep while he studied, the *maulvi* had attached a piece of string to 35 the ceiling and tied it to Parvez's hair, so if his head fell forward, he would instantly jerk awake. After this indignity, Parvez had avoided all religions. Not that the other taxi-drivers had any more respect than he. In fact, they made jokes about the local *mullahs* walking around with their caps and beards, thinking they could tell people 40 how to live while their eyes roved over the boys and girls in their care. Parvez described to Bettina what he had discovered. He informed the men in the taxi office. His friends, who had been so inquisitive before, now became oddly silent. They could hardly condemn the boy for his devotions. 45

Parvez decided to take a night off and go out with the boy. They could talk things over. He wanted to hear how things were going at college; he wanted to tell him stories about their family in Pakistan.

More than anything, he yearned to understand how Ali had discovered the "spiritual dimension", as Bettina called it.

To Parvez's surprise, the boy refused to accompany him. He claimed he had an appointment. Parvez had to insist that no appoint-
5 ment could be more important than that of a son with his father.

The next day, Parvez went immediately to the street corner where Bettina stood in the rain wearing high heels, a short skirt, and a long mac, which she would open hopefully at passing cars.

"Get in, get in!" he said.

10 They drove out across the moors and parked at the spot where, on better days, their view unimpeded for miles except by wild deer and horses, they'd lie back, with their eyes half-closed, saying, "This is the life."

This time Parvez was trembling. Bettina put her arms around him.
15 "What's happened?"

"I've just had the worst experience of my life."

As Bettina rubbed his head Parvez told her that the previous evening, as he and his son had studied the menu, the waiter, whom Parvez knew, brought him his usual whisky-and-water. Parvez was so nerv-
20 ous he had even prepared a question. He was going to ask Ali if he was worried about his imminent exams. But first he loosened his tie, crunched a poppadum, and took a long drink.

Before Parvez could speak, Ali made a face.

"Don't you know it's wrong to drink alcohol?" he had said.
25 "He spoke to me very harshly," Parvez said to Bettina.

"I was about to castigate the boy for being insolent, but I managed to control myself."

Parvez had explained patiently that for years he had worked more than ten hours a day, had few enjoyments or hobbies, and never gone
30 on holiday. Surely it wasn't a crime to have a drink when he wanted one?

"But it is forbidden," the boy said.

Parvez shrugged. "I know."

"And so is gambling, isn't it?"
35 "Yes. But surely we are only human?"

Each time Parvez took a drink, the boy winced, or made some kind of fastidious face. This made Parvez drink more quickly. The waiter, wanting to please his friend, brought another glass of whisky. Parvez knew he was getting drunk, but he couldn't stop himself. Ali
40 had a horrible look, full of disgust and censure. It was as if he hated his father.

Halfway through the meal, Parvez suddenly lost his temper and threw a plate on the floor. He felt like ripping the cloth from the table, but the waiters and other customers were staring at him. Yet he
45 wouldn't stand for his own son's telling him the difference between right and wrong. He knew he wasn't a bad man. He had a conscience. There were a few things of which he was ashamed, but on the whole he had lived a decent life.

---

to **yearn** to want sth very much

to **accompany** [əˈkʌmp(ə)ni] to go with sb
appointment *Termin*

mac *(BE)* waterproof raincoat

unimpeded *(formal)* nothing blocking
deer *Hirsch*

to **tremble** to shake because you are nervous, anxious, or cold

to **rub** *reiben*

imminent soon to take place
tie *Krawatte*
to **crunch** to chew with a crushing sound
poppadum [ˈpɒpədəm] a type of thin, round, crisp South Asian bread
to **make a face** to change the look on your face to show you disapprove of sth
harshly strictly
to **castigate** *(formal)* to criticize severely
insolent [ˈɪnsələnt] very rude, showing no respect

to **gamble** to play for money

to **wince** to suddenly make an expression with your face to show you are in pain or embarrassed
fastidious *(formal)* very critical

censure [ˈsenʃə] *(formal)* strong criticism

to lose one's **temper** to become uncontrollably angry
to **rip** to pull or tear violently

to **stand for** sth: to tolerate sth
conscience [ˈkɒnʃəns] *Gewissen*

wicked morally bad, evil

countless very many

to **relish** to enjoy • **pork pie** *Pastete mit
    Schweinefleisch*
to **deny** [dɪˈnaɪ] *leugnen* • **crispy** *knusprig*
smothered *here:* completely covered
mushroom *Champignon* • **mustard** *Senf*
fried cooked in fat in a pan
sausage [ˈsɒsɪdʒ] *Wurst*
in the village i.e. in a village in Pakistan

implicated involved

to **burp** *(informal) rülpsen*
to **choke** to be unable to breathe because
    your throat is blocked

fluently *fließend*
rowdy behaving badly
to **quell** *here:* to stop violent behaviour
infidel [ˈɪnfɪdəl] unbeliever
Christer *(slang)* a Christian
to **rout** [raʊt] to completely defeat and
    cause to flee
sink *here: Sündenpfuhl*
hypocrite [ˈhɪpəkrɪt] *Heuchler/-in*
adulterer *Ehebrecher*
persecution *Verfolgung*
jihad [dʒɪˈhɑːd] *(Arabic)* a holy war fought
    by Muslims to defend Islam

reward [rɪˈwɔː(r)d] *Belohnung*

to **urge** sb to do sth: to try hard to persuade
    sb to do sth
to **mend** one's **ways** to stop behaving badly

bill *Rechnung*
to **usher** sb **out** to lead sb out quickly
to **swallow** *schlucken*

"When have I had time to be wicked?" he asked Ali.

In a low, monotonous voice, the boy explained that Parvez had not, in fact, lived a good life. He had broken countless rules of the Koran.

"For instance?" Parvez demanded. Ali didn't need to think. As if he had been waiting for this moment, he asked his father if he didn't 5 relish pork pies?

"Well." Parvez couldn't deny that he loved crispy bacon smothered with mushrooms and mustard and sandwiched between slices of fried bread. In fact, he ate this for breakfast every morning.

Ali then reminded Parvez that he had ordered his wife to cook 10 pork sausages, saying to her, "You're not in the village now. This is England. We have to fit in." Parvez was so annoyed and perplexed by this attack that he called for more drink.

"The problem is this," the boy said. He leaned across the table. For the first time that night, his eyes were alive. "You are too implicated 15 in Western civilisation."

Parvez burped; he thought he was going to choke. "Implicated!" he said. "But we live here!"

"The Western materialists hate us," Ali said. "Papa, how can you love something which hates you?"   20

"What is the answer, then," Parvez said miserably, "according to you?"

Ali didn't need to think. He addressed his father fluently, as if Parvez were a rowdy crowd which had to be quelled or convinced. The law of Islam would rule the world; the skin of the infidel would 25 burn off again and again; the Jews and Christers would be routed. The West was a sink of hypocrites, adulterers, homosexuals, drug users and prostitutes.

While Ali talked, Parvez looked out the window as if to check that they were still in London. "My people have taken enough. If the per- 30 secution doesn't stop, there will be *jihad*. I, and millions of others, will gladly give our lives for the cause."

"But why, why?" Parvez said.

"For us, the reward will be in Paradise."

"Paradise!"   35

Finally, as Parvez's eyes filled with tears, the boy urged him to mend his ways.

"But how would that be possible?" Parvez asked.

"Pray," urged Ali. "Pray beside me."

Parvez paid the bill and ushered his boy out of there as soon as he 40 was able. He couldn't take any more. Ali sounded as if he'd swallowed someone else's voice.

On the way home, the boy sat in the back of the taxi, as if he were a customer. "What has made you like this?" Parvez asked him, afraid that somehow he was to blame for all this. "Is there a particular event 45 which has influenced you?"

"Living in this country."

"But I love England," Parvez said, watching his boy in the rear view mirror. "They let you do almost anything here."

[handwritten note: you have tooo much freedom in western countries]

"That is the problem," Ali replied.

For the first time in years, Parvez couldn't see straight. He knocked the side of the car against a lorry, ripping off the wing mirror. They were lucky not to have been stopped by the police: Parvez would have lost his licence and his job. Back at the house, as he got out of the car, Parvez stumbled and fell in the road, scraping his hands and ripping his trousers. He managed to haul himself up.

The boy didn't even offer him his hand.

Parvez told Bettina he was willing to pray, if that was what the boy wanted – if it would dislodge the pitiless look from his eyes. "But what I object to," he said, "is being told by my own son that I am going to Hell!"

What had finished Parvez off was the boy's saying he was giving up his studies in accounting. When Parvez had asked why, Ali said sarcastically that it was obvious. "Western education cultivates an anti-religious attitude." And in the world of accountants it was usual to meet women, drink alcohol, and practise usury.

"But it's well-paid work," Parvez argued. "For years you've been preparing!"

Ali said he was going to begin to work in prisons, with poor Muslims who were struggling to maintain their purity in the face of corruption. Finally, at the end of the evening, as Ali went up to bed, he had asked his father why he didn't have a beard, or at least a moustache.

"I feel as if I've lost my son," Parvez told Bettina. "I can't bear to be looked at as if I'm a criminal. I've decided what to do."

"What is it?"

"I'm going to tell him to pick up his prayer mat and get out of my house. It will be the hardest thing I've ever done, but tonight I'm going to do it."

"But you mustn't give up on him," said Bettina. "Many young people fall into cults and superstitious groups. It doesn't mean they'll always feel the same way." She said Parvez had to stick by his boy.

Parvez was persuaded that she was right, even though he didn't feel like giving his son more love when he had hardly been thanked for all he had already given.

For the next two weeks, Parvez tried to endure his son's looks and reproaches. He attempted to make conversation about Ali's beliefs. But if Parvez ventured any criticism, Ali always had a brusque reply. On one occasion, Ali accused Parvez of "grovelling" to the whites; in contrast, he explained, he himself was not "inferior"; there was more to the world than the West, though the West always thought it was best.

"How is it you know that?" Parvez said. "Seeing as you've never left England?"

Ali replied with a look of contempt.

---

rear view mirror *Rückspiegel*

to **knock** to hit with a hard blow
lorry large car used for transporting goods
wing mirror front side mirror

to **stumble** to walk unsteadily, almost falling
to **scrape** to rub by accident so that sth gets hurt
to **haul** oneself **up** to raise oneself up with great effort
to **dislodge** to forcibly remove
pitiless *mitleidlos*
to **object to** to oppose firmly

to **finish** sb **off** *here*: to be the greatest disappointment for sb

to **practice usury** ['juːʒəri] *Wucher treiben; das islamische Recht verbietet Kreditvergabe gegen Zinsen*

to **maintain** to keep up
purity ['pjʊərəti] quality of being morally upright
in the face of being confronted with
moustache [mə'stɑːʃ] *Schnurrbart*
to **bear, bore, borne** *ertragen*

prayer mat small carpet on which a Muslim goes on their knees to pray

superstitious [ˌsuːpə'stɪʃəs] *abergläubisch*
to **stick by** sb: to support sb in difficulty

to **endure** *ertragen*
to **venture to do** sth ['ventʃə] to dare to do sth
brusque [bruːsk] abrupt and rude
to **grovel to** sb *vor jdm kriechen*
inferior [ɪn'fɪəriə] not as good

seeing *here*: if we consider that

contempt *Verachtung*

inwardly in one's mind

fatiguing [fə'ti:gɪŋ] *(formal)* very tiring
haltingly hesitantly, not fluently

heartened encouraged
to **rot** [rɒt] *verrotten*
grave *Grab*

distressed upset and anxious
to **add for good measure** to give an
    additional argument

pit large, deep hole in the ground

to **oppress** sb: to treat sb unfairly and
    cruelly

morality principles concerning what is right
    and what is wrong

set hard with a fixed expression because of
    being worried or angry
mosque [mɒsk] building where Muslims
    worship

to **pull up** (a car, bus) to stop

gaudy ['gɔ:di] brightly coloured, but cheap-
    looking

One night, having ensured there was no alcohol on his breath, Parvez sat down at the kitchen table with Ali. He hoped Ali would compliment him on the beard he was growing, but Ali didn't appear to notice it. The previous day, Parvez had been telling Bettina that he thought people in the West sometimes felt inwardly empty and that   5 people needed a philosophy to live by.

"Yes," Bettina had said. "That's the answer. You must tell him what your philosophy of life is. Then he will understand that there are other beliefs."

After some fatiguing consideration, Parvez was ready to begin.   10 The boy watched him as if he expected nothing. Haltingly, Parvez said that people had to treat one another with respect, particularly children their parents. This did seem, for a moment, to affect the boy. Heartened, Parvez continued. In his view, this life was all there was, and when you died, you rotted in the earth. "Grass and flowers will   15 grow out of my grave, but something of me will live on."

"How then?"

"In other people. For instance, I will continue – in you."

At this the boy appeared a little distressed.

"And in your grandchildren," Parvez added for good measure. "But   20 while I am here on earth I want to make the best of it. And I want you to, as well!"

"What d'you mean by 'make the best of it'?" asked the boy.

"Well," said Parvez. "For a start ... you should enjoy yourself. Yes. Enjoy yourself without hurting others."   25

Ali said enjoyment was "a bottomless pit".

"But I don't mean enjoyment like that," said Parvez. "I mean the beauty of living."

"All over the world our people are oppressed," was the boy's reply.

"I know," Parvez answered, not entirely sure who 'our people'   30 were. "But still – life is for living!"

Ali said, "Real morality has existed for hundreds of years. Around the world millions and millions of people share my beliefs. Are you saying you are right and they are all wrong?" And Ali looked at his father with such aggressive confidence that Parvez would say no more.   35

A few evenings later, Bettina was riding in Parvez's car after visiting a client when they passed a boy on the street. "That's my son," Parvez said, his face set hard. They were on the other side of town, in a poor district, where there were two mosques.

Bettina turned to see. "Slow down, then, slow down!" She said,   40 "He's good-looking. Reminds me of you. But with a more determined face. Please, can't we stop?"

"What for?"

"I'd like to talk to him."

Parvez turned the cab round and pulled up beside the boy.   45

"Coming home?" Parvez asked. "It's quite a way."

The boy shrugged and got into the back seat. Bettina sat in the front. Parvez became aware of Bettina's short skirt, her gaudy rings and ice-blue eyeshadow. He became conscious that the smell of her perfume, which he loved, filled the cab. He opened the window.

While Parvez drove as fast as he could, Bettina said gently to Ali, "Where have you been?"

5 "The mosque," he said.

"And how are you getting on at college? Are you working hard?"

"Who are you to ask me these questions?" Ali said, looking out of the window. Then they hit bad traffic, and the car came to a standstill.

10 By now, Bettina had inadvertently laid her hand on Parvez's shoulder. She said, "Your father, who is a good man, is very worried about you. You know he loves you more than his own life."

"You say he loves me," the boy said.

"Yes!" said Bettina

15 "Then why is he letting a woman like you touch him like that?"

If Bettina looked at the boy in anger, he looked back at her with cold fury.

She said, "What kind of woman am I that I should deserve to be spoken to like that?"

20 "You know what kind," he said. Then he turned to his father. "Now let me out."

"Never," Parvez replied.

"Don't worry, I'm getting out," Bettina said.

"No, don't!" said Parvez. But even as the car moved forward, she 25 opened the door and threw herself out – she had done this before – and ran away across the road. Parvez stopped and shouted after her several times, but she had gone.

Parvez took Ali back to the house, saying nothing more to him. Ali went straight to his room. Parvez was unable to read the paper, 30 watch television, or even sit down. He kept pouring himself drinks. At last, he went upstairs and paced up and down outside Ali's room. When, finally, he opened the door, Ali was praying. The boy didn't even glance his way.

Parvez kicked him over. Then he dragged the boy up by the front 35 of his shirt and hit him. The boy fell back. Parvez hit him again. The boy's face was bloody. Parvez was panting; he knew the boy was unreachable, but he struck him none the less. The boy neither covered himself nor retaliated; there was no fear in his eyes. He only said, through his split lip, "So who's the fanatic now?"

---

eyeshadow *Lidschatten*
to **become conscious** [ˈkɒnʃəs] *here:* to become aware, to notice
gently kindly

to **get on** *vorankommen*

inadvertently by accident, unintentionally

fury [ˈfjʊəri] rage, extreme anger

to **pour** to put a drink in a glass or cup
to **pace** to walk determinedly

to **glance** sb's **way** to quickly look in the direction of sb
to **drag** to pull with force
to **pant** to breathe heavily with your mouth open
to **strike, struck, struck** to hit with force
none the less even so
to **retaliate** [rɪˈtælieɪt] *here:* to repay an injury
split *here:* with a bleeding cut

(handwritten notes)

Ali isn't the real fanatic here, it's Parvez

Parvez is obsessed with Ali being religious, he does not accept him

he is obsessed to a point where it gets really concerning

George Orwell (1903–1950)

Orwell was born Eric Blair in India, the son of a poorly paid civil serv-
ant in the Bengal Opium Department, in 1903. After attending Eton
in England, he spent five years serving with the Imperial Police in
Burma (1922–1927), and then several years living from hand to mouth
5 in London and in various cities in Europe. He had made up his mind to
become a writer and concentrated on observing and experiencing as
many aspects of life as he could. His early works were highly autobiographical: **Down and Out in Paris and London** (1933) and **Burmese
Days** (1934). In addition, he also produced a number of essays, includ-
10 ing **Shooting an Elephant** and **The Hanging**. With the publication
of his first books, he took the pen name George Orwell.

In 1936 Orwell became involved in the civil war that had broken out
in Spain. He fought on the side of the left-wing, loyalist Republicans
against the right-wing Nationalists, who were in rebellion against the
15 established government and who ultimately overthrew it. Orwell left
Spain within a year, recovering from a near-fatal neck wound. His war
experiences strengthened his belief in socialism and in the sacredness of the individual within a socialist
system. The war also produced in him a hatred of all forms of tyranny – whether from the right or left – as
outlined in his analysis of the Spanish war, **Homage to Catalonia** (1938).
20 After returning to England, Orwell spent his remaining years writing, raising hens and growing veg-
etables on the Hertfordshire farm he had bought with royalties from his books. Besides a number of essays
and articles for such periodicals as the *London Observer* and the New York-based *Partisan Review,* his best
known books were published in this last period: **Animal Farm** (1945), a satiric fable about Stalin and the
Soviet Union; and **Nineteen Eighty-Four** (1949), a prophetic novel about a utopia gone wrong. Orwell
25 died of tuberculosis in 1950.

Zadie Smith (1975–)

Zadie Smith was born in Willesden in the north-west London borough
of Brent in 1975 to a Jamaican mother, Yvonne Bailey, and an English
father, Harvey Smith. At the age of 14, she changed her name from Sadie
to Zadie. She attended King's College, Cambridge, where she studied Eng-
5 lish literature. Her first novel, **White Teeth** (2000), was the winner of the
Whitbread First Novel Award, the Guardian First Book Award, the James
Tait Black Memorial Prize for Fiction and the Commonwealth Writers'
First Book Award. Her second novel, **The Autograph Man** (2002), won
the Jewish Quarterly Wingate Literary Prize. Zadie Smith's third novel,
10 **On Beauty** (2005), was shortlisted for the Man Booker Prize and won the Commonwealth Writers' Best
Book Award (Eurasia Section) and the Orange Prize for Fiction. Her most recent novel is **Swing Time**
(2016). She is the editor of an anthology of short stories entitled **The Book of Other People** (2007)
and her collection of essays **Changing My Mind** was published in November 2009. Zadie Smith is a
graduate of Cambridge University and has taught at Harvard and Columbia. She is a fellow of the Royal
15 Society of Literature. Zadie Smith lives in London and is married to writer Nick Laird. The couple have
two children.

Hanif Kureishi (1954–)

Hanif Kureishi, screen writer, novelist, and film-maker, was born in Bromley, Kent in 1954. His mother was English and his father came from a family which had been displaced by the partition of India and Pakistan in 1947. Kureishi went to school in Bromley, and read philosophy at the University of Lancaster and King's College London. He enjoyed early success as a playwright and received a commission from Channel 4 to write the screenplay for what became *My Beautiful Laundrette* (1985), a film about a gay British Pakistani youth in 1980s London. It won the New York Film Critics Best Screenplay Award and an Oscar nomination for best screenplay.

5

Kureishi's first novel, **The Buddha of Suburbia** (1990), won the Whitbread Award for a first novel. Drawing on his own experiences, it focuses on a bisexual British Asian man in late 20th-century London. The novel was adapted into a television series in 1993. His second novel, **The Black Album** (1995), deals with Islamic fundamentalism and freedom of speech, and was adapted for the stage in 2009. The ideas for **My Son the Fanatic** and **The Black Album** came from the 1989 *fatwa* – a legal proclamation by an influential Islamic scholar – which condemned British-Indian writer Salman Rushdie to death and called upon Muslims to fulfil the *fatwa*. **My Son the Fanatic** was first published in the New Yorker in 1994 and made into a film in 1997 with some major changes. In 2008 Kureishi was appointed Commander of the Order of the British Empire (CBE).

10

15

Pre-reading

1. The British Empire and its legacy

1

Pair work: Read the info box below. Then write down four questions about the text to test your partner's knowledge.

The British Empire and its legacy

At its peak in the 19th century, the British Empire covered about 25% of the world's landmass. It was the largest empire in history. Britain was regarded as the "metropolis" and its colonies as the "periphery". Britain's language, literature and culture were regarded as superior to those of the colonized.

By 1970 however, most of Britain's colonies had been given political independence. The inhabitants of the colonies, whose own lives, and those of their ancestors, had been formed by the colonial experience, started to look for new ways of expressing their own political, economic and cultural ideas. So writers from the former colonies explored new ways of expressing their individuality through their literary works and showed the world the point of view of the colonized. Whereas in the past British literature had been exported throughout the world, now writing from the former colonies was imported to Britain. Famous Indian author Salman Rushdie called this phenomenon "the Empire writes back with a vengeance".

Nowadays the academic discipline of postcolonial studies scrutinizes the relationship between the colonizer and the colonized, the effects of colonialism on both the people in the colonies and in the "metropolis", and thus the changing nature of British society itself.

2

a) Give a two-minute talk on one of the following countries that belonged to the British Empire, in which you outline the country's colonial past. Refer to the beginning and end of colonialism in that country.

Canada – India – Australia – Nigeria – Egypt – Myanmar – Ireland – Sudan – Kenya – Malaysia – Jamaica – Cyprus – Hong Kong

---

b) Explain the quote: "The sun never sets on the British Empire" with reference to the talks you have listened to.

3

Read the extract taken from George Orwell's first novel *Burmese Days* (1934) on the next page, in which he portrays British colonial rule. John Flory, an Englishman who has spent most of his adult life in British India and works for a timber company, talks to his friend Dr. Veraswami, an Indian doctor.

a) Outline the two men's major arguments.

b) Compare the two men's attitudes towards the British.

c) Examine the two men's relationship.

d) Talk about the image of the colonizer and the colonized in the text.

to **thrust** to push

palsy inability to move
grave serious
septicaemia, peritonitis illnesses
paralysis inability to move
ganglia nervous system

supine stretched out
joy happiness · **bloody** (BE, informal) damn
Club place where English gentlemen used to meet
Nonconformist minister priest from a strict Protestant church
to **dodge** here: to walk, trying not to be discovered
tart (informal) prostitute
the white man's burden reference to a poem of that name by Rudyard Kipling
pukka sahib (Hindi, slang) true gentleman
sans peur et sans reproche (French) without fear and beyond reproach (Tadel); expression associated with a French knight from the Middle Ages
outrageous [aʊtˈreɪdʒəs] shocking
seditious [sɪˈdɪʃəs] encouraging rebellion
to **object to** to be against

fool idiot

to **uplift** to take to a higher level, e.g. of morality or civilization
to **rob** to steal from
to **corrupt** to make sb morally bad
sneak Kriecher/-in, Petze
to **torment** to cause terrible pain
bearable [ˈbeərəb(ə)l] OK, acceptable

"Well, doctor," said Flory – the doctor had meanwhile thrust him into a long chair, pulled out the leg-rests so that he could lie down, and put cigarettes and beer within reach. "Well, doctor, and how are things? How's the British Empire? Sick of the palsy as usual?"

"Aha, Mr Flory, she is very low, very low! Grave complications set- 5 ting in. Septicaemia, peritonitis and paralysis of the ganglia. We shall have to call in the specialists, I fear. Aha!"

It was a joke between the two men to pretend that the British Empire was an aged female patient of the doctor's. The doctor had enjoyed this joke for two years without growing tired of it. "Ah, doctor," said Flory, 10 supine in the long chair, "what a joy to be here after that bloody Club. When I come to your house I feel like a Nonconformist minister dodging up to town and going home with a tart. Such a glorious holiday from THEM"– he motioned with one heel in the direction of the Club – "from my beloved fellow Empire-builders. British prestige, 15 the white man's burden, the pukka sahib sans peur et sans reproche – you know. Such a relief to be out of the stink of it for a little while." "My friend, my friend, now come, come, please! That is outrageous. You must not say such things of honourable English gentlemen!" [...]

The doctor shook his head. "Really, Mr Flory, I know not what it 20 is that has made you so cynical. It is so most unsuitable! You – an English gentleman of high gifts and character – to be uttering seditious opinions that are worthy of the Burmese Patriot!" "Seditious?" Flory said. "I'M not seditious. I don't want the Burmans to drive us out of this country. God forbid! I'm here to make money, like every- 25 one else. All I object to is the slimy white man's burden humbug. The pukka sahib pose. It's so boring. Even those bloody fools at the Club might be better company if we weren't all of us living a lie the whole time." "But, my dear friend, what lie are you living?" "Why, of course, the lie that we're here to uplift our poor black brothers instead of to 30 rob them. I suppose it's a natural enough lie. But it corrupts us, it corrupts us in ways you can't imagine. There's an everlasting sense of being a sneak and a liar that torments us and drives us to justify ourselves night and day. It's at the bottom of half our beastliness to the natives. We Anglo-Indians could be almost bearable if we'd only 35 admit that we're thieves and go on thieving without any humbug."

2. Immigration to Britain

1

After the Second World War, a worldwide process of decolonization set in, in which Britain granted its colonies independence. Now the UK has become a country of immigration for people from its former colonies, the Commonwealth. Black and Asian people have always lived in Britain. But only since the end of World War II have they settled in Britain in greater numbers. Today they make up more than 7% of the British population.

a) Read the following text to find out about the major events in the history of Britain's immigration and race relations. The passages have all been jumbled up. Put them into the correct order.

1	2	3	4	5	6	7	8
G							

A So in the years immediately following the war, there was a large number of refugees from the Communist countries of Eastern Europe and the Soviet Union who came to Britain. Moreover, large numbers of Irish and Italians as well as so-called <u>displaced persons</u> from refugee camps all over Europe arrived in the UK.

B Hostility between different ethnic groups could sometimes lead to violence. An example is the <u>Brixton riots</u> of 1981, when black teenagers in South London expressed their anger, especially at how they were treated by the police, but also by society as a whole. The riots soon spread to other major British cities.

C Not everybody welcomed the newcomers. In the 1960s, surveys found that a majority of Britons felt that too many immigrants had been let into the country. Particularly black and Asian immigrants faced discrimination. Conservative politician <u>Enoch Powell's famous "Rivers of Blood" speech</u>, held in April 1968, can be regarded as an expression of this sentiment.

D But for the first time, there was also a significant influx of immigrants from non-European countries. One of the reasons was the <u>British Nationalities Act of 1948</u>, which granted all citizens of the Commonwealth free entry into Britain. As a consequence, Britain's non-white population grew quickly in size during the 1950s.

E Of course there has been a lot of progress, though maybe not fast enough. In 1973, Trevor McDonald became the first black newsreader. The <u>first four black members of parliament since 1922</u> were elected in 1987, and in 1993 <u>Paul Ince</u> was the first black man to captain the English national football team. Nowadays Britain is a multicultural society and the contributions of the different immigrant communities are widely recognized.

F The other major non-European immigrant group during the 1950s and 1960s was South Asians from India and Pakistan. Independence from Britain had also meant the partition of India, so these two countries formed, one with a Hindu and one with a Muslim majority population. The immigrants from this region came from very different backgrounds. They included Hindus from the west of India, Sikhs from the Punjab region and Muslims from Pakistan and what would become Bangladesh in 1971.

G After the Second World War, it was clear that immigration was needed in order to rebuild the British economy. However, the idea was that it would be mainly white Europeans, who had been the main immigrant group before the war, who would come to Britain to fill the vacancies in the job market.

H One major group of immigrants during this time was Caribbeans from the West Indies. The journey of the <u>SS Empire Windrush</u> from Kingston, Jamaica to Tilbury, Essex in June 1948 with 500 immigrants on board can be seen as the symbolic starting point of West Indian migration to the UK.

b) Choose one of the people or events that have been underlined in the text. Do some research and prepare a one-minute talk.

c) **Milling around:** Tell each other about your findings.

2

Apart from immigrants from its former colonies, Britain has also taken in refugees from outside the Common-wealth.

a) Read the box below to find out why refugees have come to Britain after World War II.

- Hungarians after the suppressed uprising in 1956
- Greek and Turkish Cypriots in the 1960s and 1970s escaping civil war
- Asians fleeing Kenya and Uganda in 1968 and 1972
- Chileans and other Latin Americans after the military coups of the 1970s
- Iranians following the 1979 Islamic Revolution
- Afghans escaping foreign invasions and civil wars from the late 1970s onwards
- Vietnamese "boat people" in the 1980s
- Sri Lankan Tamils during the civil war since the 1980s
- Turkish Kurds and Somalis following civil conflict in the 1990s
- Bosnians, Serbs, Croats and Kosovans escaping civil war in former Yugoslavia in the 1990s
- Eritreans escaping government repression, especially since 2000
- Syrians, Iraqis and Libyans fleeing from foreign invasion and civil war in the 2000s

b) **Group work:** Each group member chooses a different example from the box above and does some research on it.

c) Prepare a two-minute talk and present your topic to the other group members.

3

a) Using your results from tasks 1 and 2 on pages 40-42, draw a timeline to show when and why immigrants have come to Britain.

b) **Pair work:** Talk to your partner: What do you find striking or even surprising?

Shooting an Elephant
Pre-reading

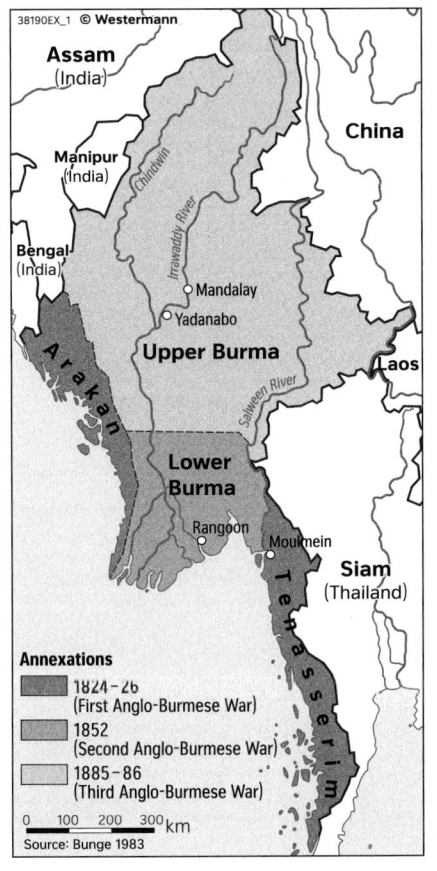

1 George Orwell
a) Read the short biography of George Orwell on page 37. Then find out more about his life and works.
b) Write an obituary for Orwell in which you use the information you have collected in a).

2 Jigsaw: British rule in Burma
George Orwell's autobiographical essay is set in Burma, today called Myanmar, where Orwell worked for the Indian Imperial Police. At that time Burma was part of British India.
a) **Home group (5):** Find out more about British rule in Burma. You can use the map on the left as a starting point. Each group member focuses on a different aspect:
   - why and how Burma became a British colony
   - the nature and organization of British rule
   - the economic aspects of British colonialism in Burma
   - the impact of colonial rule on the Burmese people
   - the main events of the colonial period
b) **Expert group:** Work together with the other students who have focused on the same aspect. Present your findings to each other and complete your notes.
c) Go back to your home group. Present your aspect of British rule in Burma to the other group members.

While reading
1
a) The story consists of 15 paragraphs. Read the summaries of the paragraphs on the next page and label them with the correct paragraph numbers (1–15). The first one has been done for you. Two summaries are missing.
b) Summarize the two remaining paragraphs and label them with the correct numbers.

Paragraph number	Summary
1	The Burmese despise the young police officer.
	He takes aim at the head of the elephant while the crowd is quieting down.
	At the scene of the incident he listens to the witnesses' reports.
	At the end the narrator reflects on the different opinions about the shooting.
	With the crowd watching him, the young police officer now feels that he is expected to shoot the elephant.
	The young police officer hates his job and British colonial rule.
	He reconsiders his plan of shooting the elephant by questioning some of the local inhabitants.
	The policeman approaches the elephant with a rifle, followed by a crowd of Burmese people.
	The young man leaves the dying animal to the inhabitants.
	He realizes that British authority will be at stake if he makes a mistake.
	One morning he is called to an incident.
	He watches the elephant, now certain that he does not want to shoot it.
	A small event gives him a deeper understanding of the way colonial government works.

Post-reading

1 The narrator

a) Collect the information about the narrator in a grid. Use three columns: a column each for
   - his situation,
   - other people's reactions to him,
   - his thoughts and feelings.

b) Choose three words from the box that describe the narrator best and explain why.

> proud – realistic – frustrated – down-to-earth – aggressive – cowardly – brave – modest – discouraged – depressed – embittered – serious – hard-headed – responsible – sensible – business-like – pragmatic

c) Analyse the narrator's character by using the information collected in tasks a) and b).

d) In the end, the narrator feels that he does not have any choice but to shoot the elephant. Do you agree? Discuss whether or not his decision is justified.

2 The Burmese people

a) Collect all the information about the Burmese people in the story.
b) Explain what the narrator thinks of the Burmese people. Give evidence from the text.
c) Use your findings from tasks a) and b) to analyse the portrayal of the Burmese people in the story.
d) Retell the story from the perspective of one of the Burmese people.

3 British colonial rule

a) **Group work:** Look at the quotes below and on the next page taken from the story and analyse the depiction of colonial rule.

Quote	Analysis
I had already made up my mind that imperialism was an evil thing and the sooner I chucked up my job and got out of it the better. Theoretically – and secretly, of course – I was all for the Burmese and all against their oppressors, the British. As for the job I was doing, I hated it more bitterly than I can perhaps make clear. In a job like that you see the dirty work of Empire at close quarters. The wretched prisoners huddling in the stinking cages of the lock-ups, the grey, cowed faces of the long-term convicts, the scarred buttocks of the men who had been flogged with bamboos – all these oppressed me with an intolerable sense of guilt.	
With one part of my mind I thought of the British Raj as an unbreakable tyranny, as something clamped down, *in saecula saeculorum*, upon the will of prostrate peoples; with another part I thought that the greatest joy in the world would be to drive a bayonet into a Buddhist priest's guts. Feelings like these are the normal by-products of imperialism; ask any Anglo-Indian official, if you can catch him off duty.	
And it was at this moment, as I stood there with the rifle in my hands, that I first grasped the hollowness, the futility of the white man's dominion in the East. Here was I, the white man with his gun, standing in front of the unarmed native crowd – seemingly the leading actor of the piece; but in reality I was only an absurd puppet pushed to and fro by the will of those yellow faces behind.	
I perceived in this moment that when the white man turns tyrant it is his own freedom that he destroys. He becomes a sort of hollow, posing dummy, the conventionalized figure of a *sahib*.	

Quote	Analysis
For it is the condition of his rule that he shall spend his life in trying to impress the "natives," and so in every crisis he has got to do what the "natives" expect of him. He wears a mask, and his face grows to fit it.	
A *sahib* has got to act like a *sahib*; he has got to appear resolute, to know his own mind and do definite things. To come all that way, rifle in hand, with two thousand people marching at my heels, and then to trail feebly away, having done nothing – no, that was impossible. The crowd would laugh at me. And my whole life, every white man's life in the East, was one long struggle not to be laughed at.	

b) The short story can be read as an autobiographical essay. This would mean that the author, George Orwell, shares the attitudes of his narrator. Accepting this view, use your findings from a) to explain Orwell's attitude towards colonialism.

c) **Pair work:** Imagine you are a journalist interviewing George Orwell about his attitude towards colonialism. Write this interview.

4 The elephant

a) Sketch the scenes in which the elephant plays a role and write captions to summarize each scene.

b) Write an analysis of the symbol of the elephant in the story. Give evidence for your interpretation by referring to the text.

The Embassy of Cambodia
Pre-reading

1 Cambodia

a) **Group work:** Do some research to find out about the history of Cambodia. Choose one or two aspects from the box below. Then give a one-minute talk to your group.

> Angkor – French protectorate – Cold War – Vietnam War – Kingdom of Cambodia (1953–1970) – Cambodian Civil War (1970–1975) – Khmer Rouge regime (1975–1979) – Vietnamese occupation (1979–1989)

b) Draw a timeline of Cambodian history. Include the events explored in task a).
c) In class, talk about the impression you have gained of Cambodia.

2 Think-Pair-Share: The title of the story

a) **Think:** You are going to read a short story called *The Embassy of Cambodia*. This is the first paragraph of the story: "Who would expect the Embassy of Cambodia? Nobody. Nobody could have expected it, or be expecting it. It's a surprise, to us all. The Embassy of Cambodia!" Speculate on the content of the short story, focusing on:
  • the setting (time and place)
  • the protagonists
  • the theme

b) **Pair:** Exchange your ideas with a partner.
c) **Share:** In class, talk about your expectations.

While reading

1

a) Summarize the content of each section in one sentence. The first two have been done for you.

Section	Summary
0 – 1	The embassy of Cambodia and its surroundings are introduced.
0 – 2	Fatou, a young African woman, passes the embassy on her way to a swimming pool, remembering how she learnt to swim in the rough Accra sea, where she worked as a chambermaid in a hotel.

Post-reading

1 Fatou

a) List the stops Fatou has made on her route to Europe.
b) Describe her work at the beach resort in Accra.
c) Collect information about Fatou's life at the Derawals' and the young Sudanese girl's life she reads about in the newspaper *Metro* (section 0 – 7). Then compare the two girls' lives. You can use the language support on the next page.

> **Language support**
>
> When comparing their lives, it is striking that …
> Unlike … it seems …
> By comparison/In comparison to/Compared to …
> By contrast/In contrast to …

d) Read the definition of modern slavery and explain it in your own words.

> Modern slavery is defined as the recruitment, movement, harbouring or receiving of children, women or men through the use of force, coercion, abuse of vulnerability, deception or other means for the purpose of exploitation. It is a crime under the Modern Slavery Act of 2015 and includes holding a person in a position of slavery, servitude, forced or compulsory labour, or facilitating their travel with the intention of exploiting them soon after.

e) Discuss to what extent Fatou is a modern slave.

2 The embassy of Cambodia
a) Collect all the information about the embassy of Cambodia given in the story.
b) Analyse the role the embassy plays in the story.
c) Use the information about Cambodia collected in the pre-reading section and discuss whether or not you think *The Embassy of Cambodia* is a fitting title for the short story.
d) Think of other possible titles and present them to the class.
e) In class, choose the best title for the short story, whether it be the original title or one you came up with in task d).

3 The game of badminton
a) Find out about the rules of badminton on the Internet: rules, faults, scoring system.
b) Explain why each section of the short story has a badminton score as a heading.
c) Analyse the symbolism of the game of badminton.
d) Discuss the meaning of the last sentence of the story.

4 The narrator
a) Collect all the information about the narrator.
b) Write a short biography of the narrator. Include information on:
   - gender
   - age
   - legal status (e.g. single, married or divorced)
   - relationship towards other people
   - job
   - personal history

   Use your findings from a) as a starting point and come up with other personal details that you find plausible.

5 Andrew Okonkwo

a) Collect information about Andrew in a grid. Include columns for:
  - his outward appearance
  - his attitudes and beliefs
  - his behaviour
  - other people's reactions to him

b) Explain what Andrew means when he says, "A tap runs fast the first time you switch it on." (p. 21, l. 26).

c) Analyse Andrew's character by using the information from tasks a) and b).

6 Silenced histories

a) Explain what the narrator means in your own words:
   "The fact is if we followed the history of every little country in this world—in its dramatic as well as its quiet times—we would have no space left in which to live our own lives or to apply ourselves to our necessary tasks, never mind indulge in occasional pleasures, like swimming. Surely there is something to be said for drawing a circle around our attention and remaining within that circle. But how large should this circle be?" (section 0 – 9, p. 15, l. 4 to p. 16, l. 5).

b) Answer the narrator's question for yourself.

c) **Group work (3):** Fatou and Andrew talk about some countries and their sad histories (section 0 – 10). Each group member should do some research on one of these events and present it to the other group members in a one-minute talk:
  - the Holocaust
  - the Rwandan genocide
  - the Hiroshima atomic bomb

d) Discuss why the author includes these historical allusions and the information about the Khmer Rouge in her story.

e) "'But more people died in Rwanda," Fatou argued. "And nobody speaks about that! Nobody!'" (p. 16, ll. 12-13). Discuss Fatou's complaint.

My Son the Fanatic
Pre-reading

1 First- and second-generation immigrants

a) Sarfraz Manzoor is a British journalist of Pakistani origin. Read the extract taken from his article "Second Generasians" (2004) and the statements on the next page (1 to 9). Decide whether they are true or false. Give evidence from the text and do not use more than eight words.

My father arrived in Britain 40 years ago. He left Pakistan, where his wife and young family remained, and travelled more than 6,000 kilometres to a cold, wet land full of pink strangers who spoke a different language. My father was just one of thousands of immigrants from the Commonwealth who left the West Indies, India and Pakistan and 5 came to Britain at the invitation of the government. The British were seeking immigrants to do work that they themselves did not want to do. The country needed factory workers, bus drivers and postmen. These and a hundred other jobs were eagerly snapped up by the new immigrants. 10

The immigrants were invited for economic reasons, and it was from an economic standpoint that the new arrivals viewed their new home. To my father, Pakistan was always going to be home, but it was England where work had taken him, and he came seeking to offer his family a better life than we might have had if we had remained 15 in Pakistan.

Coming to Britain offered new opportunities, but it also presented dangers. When you are a first-generation immigrant, it is very clear what "home" is: it is the country where you were born, raised and educated. Once the immigrants settled in Britain and had children, 20 it was inevitable that their offspring would have a more complicated relationship both with Britain and their original culture.

For people of my father's generation, the greatest fear was that their children would stop thinking of themselves as Muslim or Pakistani and instead become just Brits with brown faces. He wanted us 25 to have the best of this country, but he didn't want us to be contaminated by its worst aspects. For him, the best part was the chance to receive a first-class education and the opportunity to make something of ourselves in a country that rewarded merit and talent. It was the freedom to become what we wanted to be. The worst aspect was 30 worrying about where that freedom might lead. My father feared that we would grow up and forget that we were members of a family and not just individuals. He wanted us to be free, but not too free.

eagerly enthusiastically
to **snap up** to quickly make use of an opportunity

inevitable impossible to avoid
offspring children

to **reward** belohnen
merit good deeds or great achievements

	true	false	evidence (1-8 words)
1. The father left Pakistan together with his wife and children 40 years ago.			
2. Like thousands of other immigrants, the father was invited by the British government for economic reasons.			
3. Britain needed workers from abroad.			
4. If the father had remained in Pakistan, he could have offered his family a better life.			
5. For a first-generation immigrant, their country of origin will always be their home.			
6. The father wanted his children to become real Brits.			
7. He wanted the best education for his children and for them to have the freedom to choose what they wanted to be.			
8. He did not worry that his children would forget where they had come from.			
9. Although the father wanted his children to be free, he also worried what this freedom might lead to.			

b) Describe first- and second-generation immigrants as portrayed by Sarfraz Manzoor.
c) Explain the pun in the title of the article.

2 The Salman Rushdie affair
a) Do some research in order to write a short outline of Salman Rushdie's biography.
b) Explain the context of the 1989 *fatwah* against Salman Rushdie.

While reading

1
a) While reading, take notes on the following aspects:
  - Who are the first-generation immigrants in the story? How do they live?
  - Who are the second-generation immigrants? How do they live?
  - What are typical features of Western culture as described in the short story?
  - How are the British characterized?
  - What role does religion play in the story?
b) **Group work:** Share your findings with your group members and complete your notes.

Post-reading

1 Ali

Describe Ali's development as narrated by Parvez. The phrases in the box might help you.

> Ali used to be … – well-integrated – all of a sudden – to distance oneself from – to become radical –
> at first … then … finally …

2 An interview

a) **Pair work:** Prepare for an interview with Ali. One of you assumes the role of the journalist doing the interview, the other one the role of Ali. As the journalist, who wants to write an article about Ali, decide whether you are working for a broadsheet or a tabloid.

b) **Group work:** Form three groups:
   1. the journalists working for a tabloid: Think about who your readers are and what they might want to read about. Then think of the questions you want to ask Ali.
   2. the journalists working for a broadsheet: Think about who your readers are and what they might want to read about. Then think of the questions you want to ask Ali.
   3. the students assuming Ali's role: Think about the person Ali has become; what his situation and attitudes are. Then think of possible questions you might be asked in the interview and how you could answer them.

c) **Pair work:** With your partner from task a), do the interview. As the journalist, either record the interview or take notes for your article.

d) **Pair work:** Use your notes or recording from c) to write the article.

3 Father-son relationship

a) Choose the adjectives that best describe the relationship between Parvez and Ali. Give evidence from the short story to prove your choice.

> close – distant – unemotional – cold – warm-hearted – scornful – contemptuous – harmonious – stable –
> strained – difficult – intimate – caring – love-hate

b) Use the information from the while reading part and a) to analyse Parvez and Ali's relationship.

c) Parvez has decided to ask a therapist for advice. Host the meeting between Parvez, Ali and the therapist.
   1. Divide the class into three groups (Ali, Parvez and the therapist).
   2. In these groups, prepare for your role: In order to step into the role of the character, answer the questions below. For Parvez and Ali, use the information from the short story and invent any information not given in the story. For the therapist, come up with a plausible character profile of your own.
      - How old are you? Where do you live? Who do you live with?
      - Where do you spend most of your time?
      - What do you like doing?
      - Do you have any friends? If so, how do you spend your time with them?
      - Are you in a relationship? If so, with whom and what is the nature of this relationship?
      - What is your financial situation? What is your profession? Are you happy with it?
      - Are you happy with yourself?
      - What are your dreams?
   3. Form new groups of three (Parvez, Ali, the therapist) and perform the meeting at the therapist's.

4 Who's the fanatic now?

a) Compare these two definitions of a fanatic.

a person exhibiting excessive enthusiasm and intense uncritical devotion toward some controversial matter (as in religion or politics)	a person who has very extreme beliefs that may lead them to behave in unreasonable or violent ways

b) Find examples of fanatic attitudes and behaviour in the story.

c) At the end of the story, Ali remains passive in the face of his father's aggression. Explain why. Refer to what and why Jesus tells his followers in the Bible about "turning the other cheek" (Matthew 5:39).

d) Discuss the question at the end of the story: "Who's the fanatic now?"

5 Immigrants and their attitudes

Compare the portrayal of first- and second-generation immigrants and their attitudes in the short story with that in the article by Sarfraz Manzoor (p. 50).

Post-reading

1
Group work: Divide the class into three groups. Each group deals with one short story.
a) In your group collect important aspects of your short story that you think are worth discussing or analysing. You will find some ideas below:
- characters
- their living conditions
- topics dealt with in the short story
- problems the characters face
- setting (time and place)
- decisive events or turning points
- important quotations

b) Each group member works on a different topic. Give evidence from the text to back up your results.
c) Present your findings to your group.
d) In your group prepare a documentation poster about your short story and present it to the class.

2
Pair work: A TV station runs a special programme on immigrants and their lives. One of you is a journalist working on the programme, the other one is Fatou or Andrew from *The Embassy of Cambodia,* or Parvez from *My Son the Fanatic*. Carry out an interview and talk about
- their motives for immigrating
- how they were welcomed or accepted
- how and where they live
- what difficulties they have or had to face and how they cope(d)
- what they expect from life

Some useful literary terms

Allegory: a narrative in verse or prose form in which specific characters and actions represent abstract ideas or moral qualities. An allegory can be literal, or real, and have symbolic levels of meaning.

Alliteration: the repetition of consonant or vowel sounds at the beginning of words

Allusion: a reference to a person, place, event, or written work, such as the Bible, that the author expects the reader to recognize

Archaism: a word or expression that is out of date or old-fashioned

Climax: the turning point of the story, the crisis, after which there seems to be no other possible way for the plot to continue. The part of the plot before the climax is often called **rising action** and that after the climax is often called **falling action.**

Commentary: The author or narrator inserts his or her own comments or views.

Conflict: the clash between opposing forces. This can involve ideas, persons, the forces of nature and be internal (in the mind) or external (between two or more characters).

Diction: the choice of words used by the author to produce a certain effect on the reader

Elision: the act of omitting s.th.

Euphemism: the substitution of a mild or less negative word or phrase with a direct one, as in the use of "to pass away" instead of "to die" — can also be called **understatement**

Flashback: a scene in a story that interrupts the action to show what happened in the past

Foreshadowing: anything that hints that something, usually bad, is going to happen later

Hyperbole: an exaggeration

Imagery: vivid sensory details that arouse certain emotions or feelings in the reader

Metaphor: a direct comparison between two apparently different things, ideas, or persons without using *as* or *like*, e.g. I am a rock.

Mood: overall atmosphere of a work

Open ending: not quite a definite conclusion — there is still speculation about what might happen next.

Personification: giving human or even animal qualities to objects or things

Plot: the plan and arrangement of related incidents within a story

Plot twist: a sudden unexpected change in the direction of the plot that may lead to a surprise ending

Point of view: the manner in which the author presents the events and characters in a story
1. first-person narrator: the story is told by a character in the story, the "I" in the story – the narrator can be an adult who relates what occurred in the past as a child.
2. limited third-person narrator who focuses on one character
3. omniscient third-person or an all-knowing observer who can describe and comment about everything and everyone in the story

Protagonist: the main character in a story on whom the action centers

Register: the kind of language used in a specific social setting – Examples of register are vulgar, slang, colloquial, and formal. The kind of register used often reflects the social status of the character or may be purposely used in the wrong context or setting.

Repetition: repeating a word or phrase in a sentence to produce an effect

Setting: the location and time in which the action takes place

Simile: a direct comparison between two basically different things, ideas, or persons using *as* or *like*, e.g. She's like the wind.

Suspense: the feeling of uncertainty and anxiety as the plot rises towards its climax

Surprise ending: an unexpected ending that is not anticipated

Symbol: anything that has a meaning in itself, but also stands for something larger than itself